ANTHROPOLOGICAL PAPERS

MUSEUM OF ANTHROPOLOGY, UNIVERSITY OF MICHIGAN

NO. 54

CELTIC SOCIAL STRUCTURE: THE GENERATION OF ARCHAEOLOGICALLY TESTABLE HYPOTHESES FROM LITERARY EVIDENCE

BY

CAROLE L. CRUMLEY

ANN ARBOR

THE UNIVERSITY OF MICHIGAN, 1974

© 1974 by the Regents of the University of Michigan
The Museum of Anthropology
All rights reserved

ISBN (print): 978-1-949098-05-1
ISBN (ebook): 978-1-951519-17-9

Browse all of our books at sites.lsa.umich.edu/archaeology-books.

Order our books from the University of Michigan Press at www.press.umich.edu.

For permissions, questions, or manuscript queries, contact Museum publications by email at umma-pubs@umich.edu or visit the Museum website at lsa.umich.edu/ummaa.

PREFACE

This work has been, in many respects, an exploration of the quagmires of interdisciplinary research. Without the assistance of Paul MacKendrick (Department of Classics, University of Wisconsin), Chester Chard (Department of Anthropology, University of Wisconsin), and Frank Clover (Department of History, University of Wisconsin), its very cross-disciplinary nature might have proved fatal. This hazard was seen also by a number of colleagues in anthropology, who contributed insight, criticism and encouragement: Henry T. Wright (Museum of Anthropology, University of Michigan), Eric Wolf (Lehman College-CUNY), Stuart Piggott (Edinburgh University), Peter Carruthers (Canada Council), and William Marquardt (Washington University). Ian B. M. Ralston (Edinburgh University) offered extensive criticism of Part II, which undoubtedly has saved me from great embarrassment, but in no way shifts blame for the shortcomings of that section to him. Publication was made possible by funds from Carleton College and The University of Michigan Museum of Anthropology.

INTRODUCTION

This study presents a model of Celtic social structure, formulated from the manipulation of pertinent information on Celtic social stratification, demography, economy and trade, and settlement systems. The Celts were the major ethnic group in western Europe during what is known as the La Tène period of the Iron Age (500 B.C.-A.D. 1), inhabiting parts of the British Isles and the area which is now France. The phases immediately preceding the Roman conquest of Gaul (La Tène II and III) are of particular interest as they afford both ancient ethnographic and archaeological data at the interface of history and prehistory in Western Europe.

The initial goals of the research were threefold: (1) to initiate a long-range study of the impact of Roman colonialism on the continental Celts by first ascertaining as much as possible about Celtic society before the Roman conquest; (2) to generate hypotheses resulting from an analysis of Celtic social structure which might be tested archaeologically; and (3) to present a more rigorous technique for the integration of historiographic and archaeological data. As the study progressed, two additional goals emerged: to explore the origins of the secondary state in pre-conquest Gaul, and to explore the processual implications of information generated by the historiographic method employed here.

The discovery of these additional areas of research was not entirely serendipitous; it is with justified malaise that students of culture change have avoided the interface between the classical world and the vastly greater realms beyond. The impact of Roman imperialism on the peoples of three continents offers an excellent opportunity to isolate the mechanisms of social change, particularly acculturation. Roman society has been extensively studied and is quite well understood; it is possible, for example, to make a generalized statement on Roman economy or social structure or foreign policy. We have, to a large extent, the assistance of the Romans themselves in this task. The same types of sources exist as are used in modern studies of culture contact, namely the journals of traders, travellers, and the military, the compilation of written and unwritten information by historians of the period, and finally the archaeological evidence. Only the latter counterbalances the obvious bias of the literate classical world against the Celtic barbarians, so-called to a certain extent because theirs was an oral rather than a literary intellectual tradition.

Outside the literate classical world, subject peoples are rarely able to afford us information on their own cultures previous to Roman domination. The need to understand the barbarian cultural milieu has been dismissed with the assumption that Roman institutions were known and could be recognized with ease, and that what was not Roman was Celtic, or German, or Scythian. Despite occasional references to the similarity of some aspect of barbarian culture to that of Rome, it has been tacitly assumed by classicists and historians that such parallels were traits adopted as a result of early contact with the classical world. But such assumptions provide no answers to the question of the nature of barbarian society; they simply pose additional questions. We are still left wondering about the nature of the contact and the antecedents of barbarian culture. One cannot measure change without a reference point previous to continuous contact in each of the cultures concerned; such a reference point may be established for the Celts.

The entire process of Celtic acculturation cannot be studied at this time: we have too much Roman opinion and too little Celtic evidence. What would make feasible such a study would be a careful and accurate analysis of Celtic life before the Roman conquest: an ethnography based on the integration of archaeological and literary data. This type of analysis should, I believe, be termed paleoethnography. The more commonly used term "culture history" relies heavily on formulations based primarily on archaeological data, including material culture; similarly "ethnohistory" of necessity must often rely (with few tools to judge bias) on the evaluations of observers outside the group in question. Paleoethnography has the advantage of eliminating a great deal of bias by contrasting archaeological and literary models before attempting to integrate the two. What was left unsaid in the classical literature on the Celts is nearly as important to our understanding of Roman attitudes toward the Celts as what was commented upon.

Countless studies in many fields make admirable use of both archaeological and literary data, yet few attempt to produce a model consisting of hypotheses testable by further fieldwork, and even fewer have incorporated inconsistent data into a model. The majority of archaeological-historical studies analyze archaeological data, review pertinent historical data and produce what is essentially text-substantiated archaeological research, rather than text-modified anthropological models.

The methodology used here employs two levels of model-building: two first-level models are generated by separate analyses of literary and archaeological evidence. The literary section (Part I) introduces the special problems involved in historiography, reviews the ethnic and geographic parameters of Celtic society, attempts a critical analysis of the classical sources, and concludes with a model of Celtic social structure through the eyes of the culture which was to precipitate change in every aspect of Celtic life. The archaeological evidence (Part II) has been gathered from sites throughout Gaul (roughly the area of modern France) and the data analyzed by region. The settlement system, demography, and economy of each area has been considered, and evidence pertaining to Celtic social structure extracted to produce an archaeological model of Celtic social structure. Part III is the second level of model-building. The archaeological and literary models are compared and the emergence of general areas of accord and discord noted. Areas of discord are isolated and an attempt is made to resolve each one. In this study, discord was classified as (1) a result of identifiable biases in data-gathering, (2) a function of temporal distinctions, or (3) unresolved. Obviously, the unresolved discrepancies could not be assimilated into a composite model, but further analysis of both (1) and (2) led to the inclusion in the final model of a great deal of data usually discarded in such studies. In particular, temporal distinctions highlighted aspects of Celtic society undergoing the most rapid change. The second-level model owes its dynamism to this combination of diachronic and synchronic analyses. Part III concludes with a series of testable hypotheses concerning demography, economy, and settlement systems generated by the composite model of Celtic social structure. Appendix I traces major trends of thought on barbarian peoples, particularly the Celts. Appendices II and III contain additional archaeological data.

It should be mentioned that the use of the term "tribe" for the distinctive Gaulish ethnic groups within Celtic society is in no way related to Service's (1972: 493-96) definition of tribe; the term is used to conform to published terminology. Actually, the tribes of Gaul were more likely petty chiefdoms in a period previous to their increase in complexity.

Service (1972: 498-99), distinguishes the state level of organization from that of the chiefdom:

> States are characteristically distinguished from chiefdoms particularly, and from all the lower levels generally, by the constant threat of force from an institutionalized body of persons who wield it. A state constitutes itself *legally*: it makes explicit the manner and circumstances of its use of force, and it outlaws all other use of force as it intervenes in the disputes between individuals and groups. States tend to become differentiated from chiefdoms in other ways as well. The most striking is the cross-cutting of the society into political-economic classes. Chiefdoms have differences in individual rank, and sometimes the society is conceptually divided into two or three broad social ranks . . . but these are merely social. This differentiation is fostered by sumptuary rules; certain items of dress and ornamentation and perhaps certain kinds of food are reserved for one stratum and tabooed to another. Sumptuary rules continue in primitive states, but the classes become an aspect of political and economical differentiation as well as social. Thus the aristocracy are the state bureaucrats, the military leaders, and the upper priesthood. Other people are the producers. Full-time professionalization in arts and crafts also develops, and the artisans can be regarded as still another socioeconomic group.

Although information supporting recognition of nationally constituted Celtic authority (there is some evidence that Druids had judicial authority on a national scale) is scanty, there is little doubt that the remainder of Service's definition applies to the Celts in the period preceding the Roman conquest.

The formation of secondary primitive states may follow a pattern somewhat different than that of primary states: evidence from pre-conquest Gaul suggests that the initial evidence for state-formation is found in changes in social structure, which in turn reflect profound changes in the Celtic economy. The difficulties encountered by the Celts in their attempts to unite behind Vercingetorix were great, but they reflect a dawning political, rather than economic, national consciousness. An analysis of Celtic social structure shows that the cultural rules under which boundaries between classes were delimited changed radically in the period immediately before the Roman conquest. The initial motivation for that change came as a result of Etruscan, Greek, and Roman economic interest in the natural resources of Gaul and areas to the north, which brought considerable amounts of new capital into the Celtic economy. The functional steps from middle-man to active producer and consumer profoundly changed the determinants of class boundaries in Celtic society; Fallers' (1966) "trickle effect" (the devaluation of status goods by low status people in league with industry, with a resultant increase in competition at all levels of society), seems equally as applicable in this instance of primitive industry as in modern industrial states.

The influence of the economy in the formation of the secondary state cannot be too greatly stressed. The Germans continuously threatened Gallic peace by means of raids across the Rhine; the Cimbri and Teutons swept down into Gaul from the northeast in about 110 B.C.; yet no unification of Gaulish tribes resulted from such incursions. The Germans, Cimbri, and Teutons were no more than predatory bands, raiders who plundered and moved on. The Romans, on the other hand, obviously intended to remain. Economic response to Roman incursions became political response when the Celtic upper and middle classes found their jointly-held power base threatened. Had the Celts enjoyed a few more years of economic consolidation, the pattern of Roman domination in Western Europe might have been considerably different.

TABLE OF CONTENTS

INTRODUCTION.   v

PART I: THE LITERARY EVIDENCE

I. GENERAL RELIABILITY OF GEOGRAPHIC AND
    ETHNOGRAPHIC SOURCES   3
    Historical Criticism of Major Ancient Ethnographers and
        Geographers Dealing with the Celts   5
    Celtic Geography and Ethnic Identity   9

II. CELTIC SOCIAL STRUCTURE—LITERARY EVIDENCE 15
    Classes 15
    Other Status Determining Factors 19
    Conclusions 24

PART II: THE ARCHAEOLOGICAL EVIDENCE

III. INTRODUCTION 29
     Choice of Sites 29
     Chronology 33
     Types of Evidence 36

IV. THE ARCHAEOLOGICAL EVIDENCE 45
     North Coastal Sites 45
     West Central Sites 46
     Southwestern Sites 47

South Coastal Sites 48
Rhône Corridor Sites 61
Celtic Social Structure—Archaeological Evidence 71

PART III: GENERAL CONCLUSIONS

V. CRITICAL ANALYSIS OF LITERARY AND ARCHAEOLOGICAL
   DATA 75
   Composite Model: Celtic Social Structure 76
   Hypotheses Generated by an Analysis of Celtic Social Structure ... 77

APPENDICES

I.   Ancient Ethnographic Sources on the Celts and Their Relationships . 81

II. Additional Site Data................................ 87

III. Site Data Tables 97

BIBLIOGRAPHY 107

LIST OF FIGURES

1. Locations of Celtic groups (after Longnon: 1885) 10
2. Gaul in 58 B.C. 12
3. Gaul in the Augustan period 13
4. Map of archaeological sites, La Tène II/III, superimposed on the outline of tribal boundaries 31
5. Physiographic regions of France (after Monkhouse [1967:7]) 37
6. Cultural-geographic regions of France 39
7. Major French rivers 40
8. Pre-Roman ore deposits (after Davies [1935:76-93]) 41
9. Plan of excavations, Ensérune (28) Hérault 50
10. Plan of excavation of Entremont (30) Bouches-du-Rhône 58
11. Approximate origins of coins found at selected Celtic sites 65
12. Map of excavations at Bibracte (38) Nièvre/Saône-et-Loire 66
13. The Posidonian tradition 85
14. Maps of excavations at Kerkaradec (2) Finestère and Le Camp D'Artus (1) Finestère 89
15. Map of excavations at Gergovia (21) Puy-de-Dôme 91
16. Map of excavations at Puy-d'Issolu/Uxellodunum (24) 93
17. Gaulish walls of Uxellodunum (Roman siegeworks; Gaulish defenses) 94
18. Map of excavations at Murcens (26) 95

PART I

THE LITERARY EVIDENCE

I

GENERAL RELIABILITY OF GEOGRAPHIC AND ETHNOGRAPHIC SOURCES

THE critical evaluation of authors concerned with Celtic geography and ethnography, especially social structure, has delineated three major problem areas in classical historiography: textual problems, the authors' personal biases and measure of authority on the subject, and temporal differences in observation.

Classical texts may pose difficulties arising from differing versions of the same passage, missing or fragmentary portions of the text, errors in interpretation of translation, misquotation, or even misleading abbreviation of earlier texts. Many of these problems may be resolved by such techniques as careful comparative analysis of several manuscripts, or definition of an author's style through analysis of syntax and vocabulary; some of the problems are insoluble, and speculation on them, however learned, is destined to remain at the level of untestable hypothesis.

Delineating the areas of bias and credibility in the work of classical authors poses somewhat different problems, and allows a somewhat wider range of techniques for their solution. Attitudes toward the Celts can be broadly divided into two groups: those who looked upon them as barbarians living a life somewhat closer to nature than that of civilized men (primitivists) and those who saw the Celts as representing earlier, less desirable stages of human achievement (positivists). Except for an occasional reference to the Celts as lamentable examples of human backwardness, we would expect few positivists to have written extensively about them or any other uncivilized group; positivists much preferred to praise the advances of human society than point out its faults. Primitivists were further divided into those who praised what to them was the greater simplicity and—by inference—morality of the barbarians (soft), and those who gave the Celts no quarter but held a grudging admiration for some number of their virtues (hard). The degree of empathy of any single author for the Celts may be gauged by comparison with others who wrote on the same subject during approximately the same time period: thus works attributed to Polyhistor may be compared with those of Diodorus Siculus, or Ammianus Marcellinus to Cyril of Alexandria to obtain some indication of their personal attitudes toward barbarians in general, and the Celts in particular. Extensive discussion of these points may be found in Appendix I.

It should also be noted that general feeling toward the Celts was relatively hostile, due to the Celtic invasion of Italy in the fourth century B.C. and earlier, and of Greece and Asia Minor in the third century B.C. Another important factor which colored information on the Celts was the popularity of rhetoric, which moved both Greeks and Romans to frame artificial antitheses and defend paradoxical positions, e.g., Herodotus on Egypt, Tacitus on Germany.

Against this information must then be weighed the authority with which these individuals speak of the Celts. Biographical information on classical authors is spotty; for some authors it is quite a simple task to determine whether the writer actually observed the Celts firsthand, as did Caesar, Pliny, Ammianus, and possibly Posidonius and Tacitus, or whether he simply relied on the accounts of others, as did Lucan and Athenaeus. There is little or no biographical information on such authors as Diodorus Siculus or Timaeus, and we have little measure of their authority to speak on ethnographic or geographical matters. Reliability can be ascertained by using geography as a constant, comparing classical descriptions of a region with what is known today. In that manner, certain classical authors may be shown to be negligent (e.g., Tacitus), while others, like Strabo, are reliable and observant.

We have touched upon the variable of time with respect to information on the Celts; it is perhaps the most important consideration in the evaluation of literary evidence concerning them. The period in which most authors on the Celts wrote covers more than 500 years (ca. 115 B.C.-A.D. 395), although the primary source material was collected and written during a much shorter span (ca. 115 B.C.-A.D. 80). Yet this shorter period was the most crucial in Celtic history, because it spanned not only the Celtic move toward nationhood but also the struggle to maintain Celtic culture in the face of staggering external pressures—military, political, social, and economic—as well as such internal pressures as the abolition of kingship, redistribution of wealth, and the rivalries of various internal factions. The Celts were undergoing a period of rapid culture change during the time they were observed by classical authors, and in such periods of rapid change there is likely to be little evidence of cultural continuity, from the most exalted political alliance the nation can achieve to ambivalent allegiances of a single individual. It would be well to keep this in mind when apparent discrepancies appear in classical works regarding certain Celtic customs or attitudes or institutions. All of these were in a state of transition, and at the time of observation may have resembled neither what they had been nor what they were to become.

Despite the difficulties discussed above, there are undeniable similarities in the various accounts of Celtic ethnography and geography. At least a half-dozen had the opportunity to base what they wrote on direct personal observation (Posidonius, Strabo, Caesar, Tacitus, Ammianus Marcellinus, Pliny) independent of one another; whether or not they actually wrote from observation or relied on earlier accounts must be determined for each author individually. It is more valuable in the reconstruction of Celtic social structure to examine each item of information in turn, evaluating the credentials of its author, the political and social implications of its subject matter, and its relationship to the changes Celtic society underwent in the last centuries of the Republic and the first century of the Empire.

HISTORICAL CRITICISM OF MAJOR ANCIENT ETHNOGRAPHERS AND GEOGRAPHERS DEALING WITH THE CELTS

Although the formulation of hypotheses concerning traditions of hard and soft primitivism (see Appendix I) helps to explain major trends in sentiment among the classical authors who mention the Celts, it is nonetheless necessary to evaluate critically to the extent of our knowledge the attitudes, the motives, and the authority of those individuals who might prove most influential in a reconstruction of Celtic social structure. Three of those whose reports bear particular weight (Caesar, Strabo, Diodorus) were apparently quoting directly from Posidonius (ca. 135-ca. 50 B.C.), considered the most important Stoic philosopher and ethnographer of his time (Chadwick, 1966:xix-xx). He was born on the Orontes, studied philosophy at Athens, and became a teacher at Rhodes, where he was known to Cicero. He travelled widely and made scientific investigations throughout the Western Mediterranean, including Gaul (OCD:1968). Tierney (1960:198) comments that the Celtic ethnography of Posidonius represents the highest level of achievement, not only in Celtic ethnography but in Greek ethnography as a whole. His stated method (as reported in Strabo, I.2, 34) was "to search for the true origins by studying the common qualities and family likenesses of nations" (*ibid.* 201); his criteria were language, way of life, bodily characteristics, geographical distribution, common names, all considered under the transforming influences of climate and lapse of time acting toward assimilation or dissimilation. One could hardly ask for a more sophisticated and modern methodology. Yet since Posidonius' work survives only in other authors, his hypothetical reliability is somewhat at the mercy of those who preserve him. Comparative analysis of sections of Athenaeus, Diodorus, Strabo, and Caesar of suspected Posidonian origin has yielded a consistent method, style, and vocabulary which must have been very close to Posidonius' original text. Yet the particular portions that were selected from the original text and the manner in which they were summarized are in some cases particularly revealing of the individuals utilizing Posidonius.

Athenaeus (fl. ca. A.D. 200) quotes verbatim a long passage on Celtic food and drink, reflecting, no doubt, Athenaeus' own interests: the passage occurs in *The Learned at Dinner*. Passages on Celtic social and political organization, also from Posidonius, are most useful and appear to quote the earlier source verbatim (Tierney, 1960:222).

Diodorus Siculus (fl. 60-30 B.C.) extracts passages on Celtic geography and ethnography from Posidonius and embellishes them with a few ill-advised additions of his own. The additions are not as problematical as Diodorus' ruthless abbreviation of the original (Tierney, 1960:204). There is no evidence that he travelled in Gaul.

Strabo (64-3 B.C.-A.D. 21) knew Posidonius and used his work extensively for his own geography and ethnography of Gaul. A Greek geographer and historian, Strabo had included Gaul in his extensive travels. His work and interests as expressed in his *Geographia* reflect his abiding allegiance to Stoicism (Dubois, 1891:385). He was an innovator in geographical methodology, and although somewhat negligent in composition and style, his logical approach to diverse subjects and his continuation of the scientific tradition of Eratosthenes and Hipparchus make his work valuable, if subject to qualified criticism in the nature of personal bias.

> ... In addition to their witlessness they possess a trait of barbarous savagery which is especially peculiar to northern peoples, for when they are leaving the battle-field they fasten to the necks of their horses the heads of their enemies, and on arriving home they nail up this spectacle at the entrances to their houses ... they used to stab a human being whom they had devoted to death, in the back with a dagger, and foretell the future from his convulsions. ...
>
> (IV, IV.5)

Tierney (1960:211) points out that both Strabo (in the above quotation) and Caesar (*BG*, 6, 16) repeat an attack on the Celts mentioned in Posidonius. Celtic vanity and boastfulness are illustrated, followed by documentation of their barbarous inhumanity as exemplified in the practices of headhunting and divination by human sacrifice. This use of Posidonius by Strabo and Caesar in the manner of the hard primitivists underscores the continued existence of the Posidonian tradition into the time of the Empire. However, as Lovejoy and Boas (1935) suggest, Posidonius was "hard" because he was early and the Celts were still relatively new and strange to Mediterranean peoples; Strabo and Caesar have no such excuse, and in the case of both we are dealing with a rather obvious personal bias against the Celts.

The historical reliability of Julius Caesar (100-44 B.C.) has only recently become of major interest to classicists and historians, partially as a result of the more culturally relativistic approach used by anthropologists and historians of science. Tierney (1960:211 ff.) and Rambaud (1953) make a strong case for Caesar's manipulation of his information on the Celts to fit his own political ends. His political situation in 53 B.C., when he wrote the ethnographic part of the *Commentaries* (*BG*, 6), was not particularly stable nor was his military situation in the field firmly in hand: he had narrowly avoided disaster when the Aedui bolted his armies and joined the Gaulish national resistance. It has been suggested that Caesar's sections on ethnography served to divert the Senate's notice from his defeats in the field, and that the publication of the *Commentaries* themselves produced needed propaganda reflecting well on his exploits. It is unlikely that Caesar had any clear conception of the ideas of Posidonius, but he was astute enough to be impressed by Posidonius' work (Tierney, 1960:213). Caesar was completely disinterested in Celtic ethnography, and only considered those of high rank in Celtic society worth discussion. These individuals were, of course, also of interest to Caesar politically and this above all governed his choice of topics on the Celts. He half-heartedly included some Celtic customs, probably because he knew such sketches were an accepted part of historiography, but his main emphasis is on Celtic political organization presented in a manner suiting his own propagandistic purposes. Caesar's only attempt at a viewpoint independent of that of Posidonius is the differentiation of the Celts from the Germans, based on knowledge which had been recently acquired. This, too, suited his political ends, as the Rhine was a barrier limiting the theater of the war, and the peoples to the east of it were Caesar's ultimate raison d'etre in Gaul.

Tierney (1960:222) has summarized the four authors most heavily indebted to Posidonius as follows: Athenaeus gives a few points of Posidonius nearly verbatim, Diodorus abbreviates ruthlessly and omits important sections but most nearly approximates the succession of themes in Posidonius, and Caesar finally omits everything which is not of political interest. Strabo's personal opinions undoubtedly color his choice of information but he fills in important gaps in Posidonius' Celtic ethnography.

Of those remaining authors who speak at length of Celtic social organization, only Lucan (A.D. 39-65) is also of the Posidonian tradition. A Roman of Spanish origin, he was educated in Rome, embraced Stoicism, and published in 10 books his epic, the *Pharsalia*. He was put to death under Nero, leaving unfinished his epic on the Civil War between Pompey and Caesar. The chief sources for Lucan's poetry were Livy and probably Caesar himself. For example, Lucan refers in the *Pharsalia* to a sacred woods where the Druids dwelt and practiced barbaric rites and a sinister mode of worship (*Pharsalia*, i.450 ff.). Of a grove near Marseille he says, "The people never frequented the place to worship very near it, but left it to the gods . . . the priest himself dreads the approach and fears to come upon the lord of the grove" (*Pharsalia*, iii.422 ff.). The worship of the gods was practiced, writes Lucan, "with barbaric rites, the altars heaped with hideous offerings, and every tree sprinkled with human gore" (*Pharsalia*, iii.399 ff., translated by Chadwick, 1966:36-7). Nutting (1934:291 ff.) has effectively pointed out Lucan's use of vagueness and half-truths to create a striking effect, yet he suggests that it is only fair to judge him by the standards of his time. While this may be so from a literary standpoint, it must render suspicious any scientific use of Lucan as a source of Celtic ethnographic information.

Tacitus (A.D. 55-120) was a distinguished Roman historian biased strongly in favor of the barbarian nations—a soft primitivist. He quite possibly spent his early years in northeastern Gaul (Church and Brodribb, 1868:vii). As an historian, he has several obvious defects: he is careless about geography and military history, and is not without a certain ironic arrogance (Mattingly, 1948:10). He often pleads his case for the barbarians somewhat more elegantly than believably, and perhaps should be considered more a rhetorician than an historian.

Dio Chrysostom (ca. A.D. 40-120) was demonstrably of the Alexandrian tradition, and a contributor to our information on Celtic social organization. He was an eminent Greek sophist and rhetorician under the Roman Empire, converted to Stoicism rather late in life. We have little evidence from which to evaluate his work critically.

Very late sources of evidence, such as Ammianus Marcellinus (A.D. 330-395) and Cyril of Alexandria (fl. A.D. 412-444), are doubly difficult to evaluate, so removed were they from the time period of our interest in the Celts. Both Cyril and Ammianus apparently used such earlier sources as Polyhistor and Timagenes, to which we have access only in fragmentary form. Ammianus shared with the earlier great Roman historians a certain taste for autobiographical reference and we have a great deal of information on his life and works. Considered the last of the Roman historians of stature, he was in some respects better prepared to report the affairs of the Empire than a relatively sheltered individual like Tacitus: Thompson (1947:125) notes Ammianus' active military service, and compares it to that of Tacitus, who "languished for a few years in the passive defense of a quiet Frontier." Ammianus appealed strongly to upper and middle class readers; his own middle class origins may have made him identify himself somewhat less with the aristocracy than did earlier historians. His style was cumbrous and obscure, but never dull, and his ability to characterize was unequalled even by Tacitus (Thompson, 1947:124). However, his geography in certain cases is inaccurate (*ibid.*:4).

Pliny the Elder (A.D. 23/4-79) was perhaps the most generally reliable of the authors who wrote on the geography of Gaul. He served in Germany and in Gaul, and collected firsthand data; his reputation for diligence, accuracy, and rationality is as well known now as it was among his contemporaries.

In many respects, Pliny exemplified the more desirable qualities of classical authors whose works are used in critical historiography. A great deal is known about Pliny's attitudes, his travels, and the social and political climate of the age. The historical bias of an author may best be analyzed when three factors are known: whether the writer had firsthand knowledge, or based his impressions on the works of others; what his personal bias was with reference to barbarian peoples; and certain aspects of the political and social milieu in which he wrote.

CELTIC GEOGRAPHY AND ETHNIC IDENTITY

By the time of Herodotus (ca. 484-424 B.C.) the Greeks recognized the Celts as a major barbarian people living west and north of the western Mediterranean, and beyond the Alps. Through the literature, their presence there is documented to at least the sixth century B.C. Their initial identification as Celts (their own word for themselves) seems to have been based on a characteristic way of life, political organization, and appearance. As Powell (1958:17) points out, Greeks seldom learned foreign languages, so linguistic differentiations among the Celts would not have come under Greek consideration. Thus, in all probability the Celts as an ethnic entity were often identified by group names. This is, to modern ethnographers, a rather shaky foundation, but as Tierney (1960:199) points out:

> . . . it is necessary to realize that the distinct ethnographic unit is rather like the chameleon, that in fact, strictly speaking, such entities do not exist. How many of the numerous natural and artificial elements in the units are in any way lasting, apart from the physiological bases of the genes?

He goes on to remind the reader that Western Europe underwent rapid cultural change throughout the classical period; cookery was as fluid as kingship or architecture or burial rites.

An ethnographic unit is a dynamic model; this is an important concept to keep in mind when dealing with ethnographic information gathered over at least a 500-year period. Perhaps the best guidelines are the attitudes of the Celtic peoples themselves about whether they were a functioning social and political unit. This is the most common criterion of the classical writers; they relied primarily on the groups' names for themselves.

More explicit location and identification of Celtic groups discussed in the classical texts is best made by reference to the authors themselves. Of those who deal with Celtic geography, five authors give us detailed information: Strabo, Diodorus Siculus, Pliny the Elder, Caesar, and Ammianus Marcellinus.

Diodorus Siculus, Caesar, and Strabo recognized that *Galli* and *Galatae* were equivalent names for *Keltoi/Celtae,* and Caesar is quite definite (*BG.* I.i) on the point that the Galli of the first century B.C. knew themselves by the name

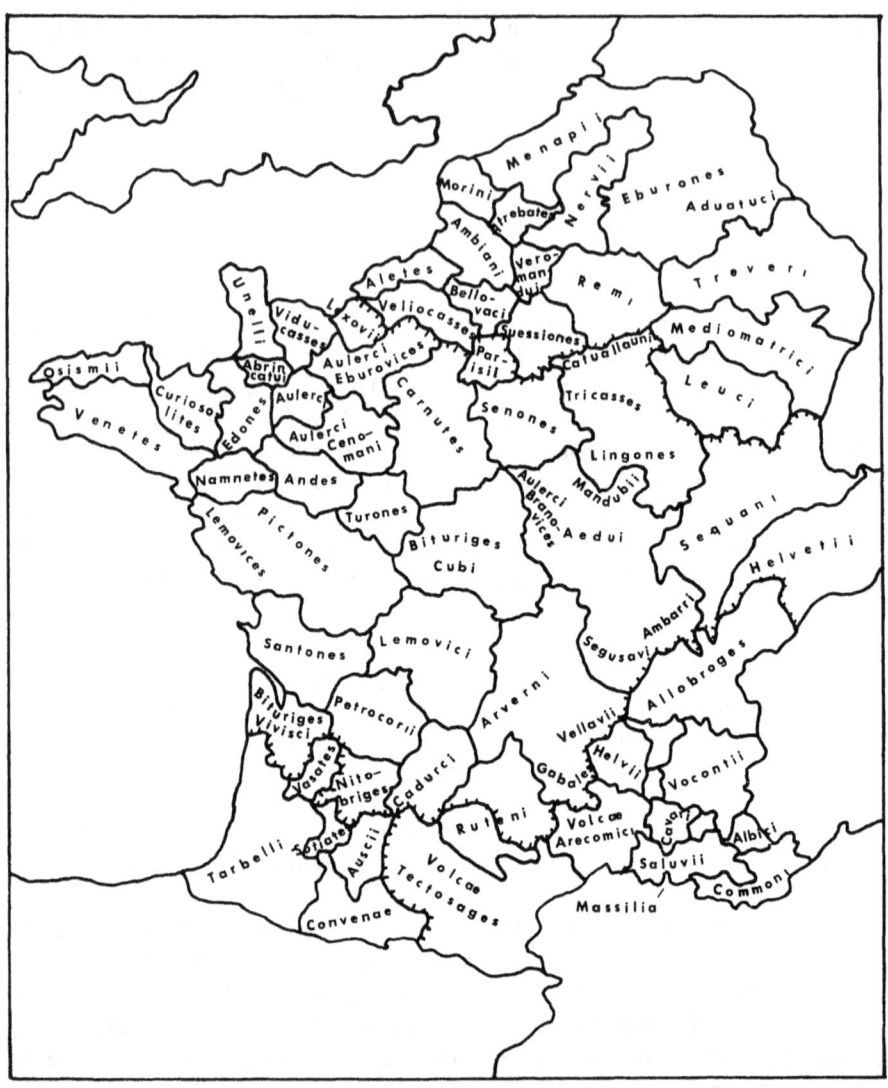

(from Longnon, *Atlas Historique de la France depuis César jusqu'a nos jours*, 1885)

Fig. 1. Gaulish Tribal Boundaries.

Celtae. Diodorus used the names indiscriminately, but considered Keltoi the more correct; Strabo says the word was known to the Greeks because of the Celts living inland from Massilia. Powell (1958:21) says it is probably impossible to unravel the names at this point. It might be that one may have initially referred to a tribal (Galli?) and the other (Celtae?) to a regional designation. As has been noted, classical observers were uninterested in the niceties of barbarian linguistics. Diodorus (fl. 60-30 B.C.) recounts a more probable explanation for the ambivalent use of Gauls and Celts to describe the inhabitants of the region under consideration:

> And now it may be useful to draw a distinction which is unknown to many: the peoples who dwell in the interior above Massilia, those on the slopes of the Alps, and those on this side of the Pyrenees mountains are called Celts, whereas the people who are established above this land of Celtica in the parts which stretch to the north, both along the ocean and along the Hercynian mountain, and all the peoples who come after these as far as Sythia, are known as Gauls; the Romans, however, include all these nations together under a single name, calling them one and all Gauls.
> (V.32.1)

Caesar's description of Celtic geography, written in 53 B.C., has become a classic; not only is his geographic material based on personal observations gathered on his campaigns, but his clarity and deceptive simplicity of style have long been textbook samples of Latin grammar. The passage begins his *Gallic Wars:*

> Gaul is a whole divided into three parts, one of which is inhabited by the Belgae, another by the Aquitani, and a third by a people called in their own tongue Celtae (in the Latin Galli). All these are different from one another in language, institutions and laws. The Galli (Gauls) are separated from the Aquitani by the river Garonne, from the Belgae by the Marne and the Seine. . . . The separated part of the country which, as has been said, is occupied by the Gauls, starts from the river Rhône, and is bounded by the river Garonne, the Ocean, and the territory of the Belgae; moreover, on the side of the Sequani and the Helvetii, it touches the river Rhine; and its general trend is northward. The Belgae, beginning from the edge of the Gallic territory, reach to the lower part of the river Rhine, bearing towards the north and east. Aquitania, starting from the Garonne, reaches to the Pyrenees and to that part of the Ocean which is by Spain; its bearing is between west and north.
> (I.1)

Strabo (63 B.C.-A.D. 21) describes Celtic holdings as follows:

> . . . Keltica . . . extends as far as the Rhine. Its northern side is washed by the entire of the British Channel, for this island lies opposite and parallel to it throughout, extending as much as 5000 stadia in length. Its eastern side is bounded by the river Rhine, whose stream runs parallel with the Pyrenees; and its southern side commencing from the Rhine, [is bounded] partly by the Alps, and partly by Our Sea; where what is called the Galatic Gulf runs in, and on this are situated the far-famed

Fig. 2. Gaul in 58 B.C.

REALIABILITY OF GEOGRAPHIC AND ETHNOGRAPHIC SOURCES

Fig. 3. Gaul in the Augustan Period.

> cities of Marseilles and Narbonne. Right opposite to the Gulf on the other side of the land lies the Gulf, called by the same name, Galatic, looking toward the north and Britain. It is here that the breadth of Keltica is narrowest, being contracted into an isthmus less than 3000 stadia but more than 2000. Within this region there is a mountain ridge, named Mt. Cevennes, which runs nearly at right angles to the Pyrenees, and terminates in the central Plains of Keltica.
>
> (2.5.28)

Generally, he followed Caesar on the boundaries and divisions of tribes in Gaul, as his personal acquaintance with the area was comparatively superficial (Bunbury, 1879:247). His description of Provincia Narbonensis was, however, minute and accurate and suggests considerable personal familiarity.

Aquitania increased considerably in size under Augustus, a move to make the three provinces roughly equivalent for administrative purposes; thus; the boundary between Celtica and Aquitania was moved from the Garonne River to the Loire River (see Figs. 2 and 3).

The mid-first century work on Gaul of Pliny the Elder is probably the most complete of the surviving texts, adequately summing up other authorities and tempered with his own observations and diligence. To previous discussions of the main boundaries of Celtic lands, he added detailed information on the location of individual tribes, and listed them as belonging either to Belgic, Celtic, or Aquitanian Gaul (IV, xvii-xix). From Caesar, Strabo, and Pliny, a map of the locations of the tribes and their approximate boundaries (Longnon, 1885) has been constructed (Fig. 1).

Ammianus Marcellinus was in Gaul himself between A.D. 354 and 359, attached to the staff of Ursicinus. His description of Celtic boundaries does not differ from those already discussed. He does mention that the three major Celtic divisions "differ in language, habits and laws" (XV, 11.2,3-18).

II

CELTIC SOCIAL STRUCTURE—LITERARY EVIDENCE

THE foregoing historiographic analysis of authors who wrote about the Celts allows construction of a model of Celtic social structure based solely on the literary evidence. In subsequent chapters the literary model will be compared and contrasted with the archaeological model and a composite model will be presented.

CLASSES

The Aristocracy: *Druides, Equites*

On the basis of socioeconomic distinctions, literary evidence suggests that Celtic society consisted of two classes: the aristocracy and the commoners (Caesar's *Druides* and *equites,* and *plebs*). Caesar distinguished only the aristocracy (Druides and equites) as being worthy of further attention, as they alone controlled Celtic social, political, and religious life. Of Druids, he says (*De Bello Gallico,* 6.13) their functions are religious, educational, and legal. Information from sources other than Caesar (see Chadwick, 1966; Tierney, 1960 for summaries) suggests that one had to be a member of the aristocracy to be a Druid, but that perhaps not every aristocrat was a Druid. Obviously, since the training of a Druid often took as long as 20 years (Caesar, *BG,* 6.13), those who were students must have been removed from the mainstream of public life for a large part of that time.

Caesar also says (*BG,* 6.14) that Druids were exempt from taxation and took no part in warfare. It may be that all young aristocratic Gaulish men took some Druidic training; other information suggests that an aristocracy existed apart from the more parochial activities of the Druids. It would appear that, in any event, the function of the aristocracy was predominantly administrative. Grenier (1945:183, 216) suggests that the aristocracy was only a few generations old at the time of the conquest, that it replaced a system of royalty which fell under the pressure of a class whose wealth increased through trade with the classical world; thus, more individuals shared in the control of the economy and status differentiations were multiplied. Although the origins and functions of Celtic kingship are hotly disputed, the above does remain a plausible explanation for the continued presence of "kings" among the British Celts and Celts in Aquitania and Belgica. Caesar understood the reason for the abolition of kingship among the Celtae in central Gaul to be the result of an increase and abuse of the system of clientship (to be discussed further below). Factions of the aristocracy in either case would have found themselves strong enough to abandon higher allegiances.

By far the most influential group in Celtic life—politics, social structure, religion—was the Druids. They were part of a group of specially trained individuals, generally men, drawn from the aristocratic class. Caesar says (*BG*, 6.13.14):

> Druids are concerned with divine worship, the due performance of sacrifices public and private and the interpretation of ritual questions; a great number of young men gather about them for the sake of instruction and hold them in great honor. In fact, it is they who decide in all disputes, public and private; and if any crime has been committed, or murder done, or there is any dispute about succession or boundaries, they also decide it, determining rewards and penalties: if any person or people does not abide by their decision, they ban such from sacrifice, which is their heaviest penalty.
>
> (trans. H. J. Edwards)

> The Druids usually hold aloof from war, and do not pay war taxes with the rest; they are excused from military service and exempt from all liabilities. Tempted by these great rewards, many young men assemble of their own volition to receive their training; many are sent by their parents and relatives. Report says that in the schools of the Druids they learn by heart a great number of verses, and therefore some persons remain twenty years under training. And they do not think it proper to commit these utterances to writing, although almost in all other matters, and in their public and private accounts, they make use of Greek letters. I believe that they have adopted the practice for two reasons—that they do not wish the rule to become common property, nor those who learn the rule to rely on writing and so neglect the cultivation of the memory; and, in fact, it does usually happen that the assistance of writing tends to relax the diligence of the student and the action of the memory. The cardinal doctrine which they seek to teach is that souls do not die, but after death pass from one to another; and this belief, as the fear of death is thereby cast aside, they hold to be the greatest incentive to valor. Besides this, they have many discussions as touching the stars and their movement, the size of the universe and of the earth, the order of nature, the strength and powers of the immortal gods, and hand down their lore to the young men.
>
> (trans. H. J. Edwards)

Diodorus makes the following observations (v.31.2-5):

> Among them are also to be found lyric poets whom they call Bards. These men sing to the accompaniment of the instruments which are like lyres and their songs may either be of praise or of obloquy. Philosophers, as we may call them, and men learned in religious affairs are unusually honored among them and are called by them Druids. The Gauls likewise make use of diviners, accounting them worthy of high approbation, and these men foretell the future by means of the flight or cries of birds and the slaughter of sacred animals, and they have all the multitude subservient to them ... and it is a custom of theirs that no one should perform a sacrifice without a philosopher, for thank-offerings should be rendered to the gods by the hands of men who are experienced in the nature of the divine ... in wars as well as peace they obey these men and their chanting poets ... many times when armies approach each other with swords drawn and spears thrust forward, these men step forth between them and cause them to cease....

Lucan (*Pharsalia*, I, 11. 449-462) and Strabo (*Geographia*, 4.4.4) make similar observations. Three functional distinctions were made: the bards composed and chanted hymns; the *vates* or prophets gave sacrifices and studied nature in an effort to presage; the Druids were moral philosophers and the embodiment of justice in the Celtic community.

It is unclear in Caesar whether bards, prophets, and philosophers were all Druids, or whether only philosophers were. Strabo (*Geographia*, 4.4.4) describes them all as men held in exceptional honor, but refers only to the philosophers as Druids. Chadwick (1966, viii) classifies the three groups as subdivisions of the Gaulish intellectuals, but refers only to the philosophers as Druids.

The functions of the bards were, curiously, much like those of the medieval minstrel: to entertain, to inform, and to exert social pressure using wit and ridicule. The vates, or prophets, functioned more in a magico-religious mode, presiding over the mysteries of nature, sanctifying momentous occasions through ritual, foretelling the future through divination. The Druids, whom Ammianus Marcellinus (XV, 9.8) distinguishes as loftier in intellect than the others and bound together in fraternal organizations, had extensive powers over other Celts and apparently controlled Celtic government. Dio Chrysostom (49th Discourse, 8) says:

> The kings were not permitted to do or plan anything without the assistance of these wise men, so that in truth it was they who ruled, while the kings became their servants and the ministers of their will, though they [the kings] sat on golden thrones, dwelt in great houses, and feasted sumptuously.
>
> (trans. H. L. Crosby)

Caesar mentions (*BG*, 6.13) that the Druids, at a certain time of the year, met within the borders of the Carnutes (near Chartres), whose territory was reckoned at the center of Gaul, and sat in conclave in a consecrated spot to give lawful trial in disputes. Caesar also refers to the extensive teaching activities of the Druids.

The most commented-upon characteristic of the Druids was their moral philosophy: they taught that there was indeed an afterlife in which debts were payable and one could partake of both business and pleasure. The concept that the soul was immortal fascinated classical writers, and comparisons were made between Druidic philosophy and the other major bodies of world philosophical thought: Egyptian, Assyrian, Persian, Indian (Cyril of Alexandria, *Contra Julianum*). Diogenes Laertius (*Vitae*, I.1, 1.5) reports that many thought the study of philosophy began among the barbarians. Lucan (*De Bello Civili*, I, 11. 449-462) says the Celtic valor in battle is due to their belief in the immortality of the soul and their conviction that it is cowardly to be careful of a life which will come back. It is interesting and important to note that in the same passage Lucan mentions ". . . the Druids, laying down their arms, went back to . . . their worship" which contradicts Caesar's statement (*BG*. 6.13) that Druids do not bear arms. The disagreement may be minor, but serves to remind us of the fallibility of our sources. Lucan was after all a poet, and the comment rhetorical; the fact that the Gaulish revitalization leaders—Dumnorix and Cicero's friend and Aeduan chief, Divitiacus—were Druids suggests misinformation on Caesar's part. The role of Druid would seem to have been less strictly defined than Caesar would have us think. In the attempt to type and classify, perhaps the flexibility of the organization was overlooked.

The classical information on the Druids, the bulk of which is in Caesar and a few other writers who were probably indebted to Posidonius, may be summarized as follows: the Druids had a reputation outside Gaul as early as the second century B.C.; in Caesar's time they were an organized and powerful body having important educational, judicial, political, and religious functions. The order included various officials, priests, prophets, and poets. Apparently some of its members were free to devote themselves entirely to the duties of government and international affairs. Their primary effect was to concentrate political, social, and religious power at the top of Celtic class structure, among the aristocracy.

The Druidic and the knightly or warrior class formed the aristocracy. The functions of the knightly class were political and military; they shared the first with the Druids and reserved the second as their primary duty. They alone commanded in wartime, according to Caesar. Relative to his importance in terms of birth and resources, each knight gathered about him a number of liegemen and dependents. Nicholas of Damascus, quoted by Athenaeus (6.249B), refers to the knights of the Celtic tribe Sotiani (unknown by Caesar's time?) as *siloduri*— bound by a vow—to live and die for their king and, less stringently, to maintain economic support pledged their clients, the commoners.

Commoners: *Plebs*

The mass of people, according to Caesar (*BG*, 6.13) "are reduced to a condition resembling slavery, without rights and without any participation in affairs.

Overwhelmed by the weight of debts and taxes, victims of the violence of the aristocracy, they themselves voluntarily passed into servitude to the nobles" (trans. C. L. Crumley).

Rambaud (1953) suggests that Caesar misrepresented the lot of the plebs for two possible reasons: to curry favor with debt-ridden Roman plebs, and to scare the Roman Senate into continuing support for his campaign. Desjardins (1885), however, points out that the situation of the people as seen by Caesar in these two passages seems to refer to an earlier epoch; for during the eight years Caesar was among the Celts an internal revolution was taking place. The political inequities of the people were profoundly modified in the time of Vercingetorix (Gaulish national leader and military adversary of Caesar). Son of a king, he himself was probably not the democratic leader modern French patriots would have him be; on the other hand, the common cause of Gaulish independence undoubtedly had a confusing effect on long-standing class distinctions. The Gaulish aristocracy was divided in its loyalty to Rome or to independent Gaul; a change in patrons would conceivably change the outcome of a battle or of the entire campaign. The function of the plebs was the function of commoners everywhere: to provide the economic base for the entire society. Yet they were not powerless over their own destinies, as one might reasonably expect: a client was able to create leverage in his personal situation by prudent use of the threat to change patrons.

OTHER STATUS DETERMINING FACTORS

Patron-Client Relationships

A powerful ingredient in determining Celtic class divisions, just as in Roman practice, was the institution of clientage; it appears to have been the major delineator of the relationship between the aristocracy and the commoners. Wolf (1966) has analyzed the patron-client relationship in functional terms: the patron offers economic assistance and the protection from legal and illegal authority, while the client offers demonstrations of esteem, information on the machinations of others, and the promise of political support. Apparently, both Druides and equites served as patrons of the lower class.

The institution of clientage was the basis of Celtic political organization. The earliest mention of clientship among the continental Celts is by Polybius (in *Historia*), who describes the advantages to a Gaulish noble of a number of retainers and clients (2.17); Caesar also notes its mutual advantages (6.15.2). Of course, the institution itself has a lengthy history among many Indo-European peoples: Posidonius identifies a similar institution among the Thracians, the Germans, and the Aryans of India (Mauss, 1926). Grenier (1945:220) remarks that one cannot exaggerate the importance of clientship in Gaul, as it was the major source of power of such leaders as Orgetorix and Dumnorix. Other systems may have relied primarily on the solidarity of the gens (descent group); among the Celts the *familia* of a Celtic chieftain, his relatives and retainers, was of greater importance. The word Polybius uses to describe the relationship is "brotherhood," which tempts comparison with modern Sicilian social structure. "Tout ce regime repose sur un systeme quasi féodal de clientèle" (Grenier, 1945:180). The control of the aristocracy over the plebs, who were organized in such towns as Bibracte and Alesia, particularly foreshadows the Middle Ages. According to Grenier (1945:214), there was a master of Uxellodunum (Puy d'Issolu), and under the aegis of that individual, artisans and merchants alike plied their trade.

Wolf (1966:17) points out that patron-client relations are particularly active where the formal institutional structure is weak and unable to deliver steady goods and services to lower levels of the social order. The comment was made with reference to such relationships within a modern governmental complex; in the Celtic example, the growing strength of the patron-client relationship may well have been leading to a more sophisticated political organization.

Land Tenure

Another institution which has great bearing on the status of Celtic commoners is land tenure. Whether the concept of individual ownership of property or collectivization was present in pre-Roman times has been discussed at length by the major Celtic scholars. D'Arbois de Jubainville (quoted in Grenier [1945]) believes collective property to have been unknown among the Celts by the time of Caesar. Jullian and Fustel de Coulanges thought they had found in Caesar evidence of the existence of private property. Hubert concludes that both types existed among the Celts in the time of Caesar (Grenier, 1945:215). Yet another possibility is that extended families were the landowners, and particular plots were let out to family members on the basis of status. It is my feeling that too little information is available to determine the nature of property ownership. The Orange Cadaster (a taxation record for the city of Orange, in southeastern France) shows individual Gallic ownership ca. A.D. 70, but it is impossible to relate this fact to the pre-conquest period.

De Jubainville assumes that in earlier times the Celts had arrived as conquerors, and the land they took became a part of the public domain. Polybius (II, 17) says that the major sources of Celtic wealth were gold and cattle, so we may assume these commodities to have been (generously?) distributed among the aristocracy. De Jubainville argues that it was to the advantage of the aristocracy to maintain communal lands on which to graze their cattle. As added insurance, they would have controlled the material means for working the land:

tools, seeds, manpower. Only after the Roman conquest and the extension of the domain of Gallo-Roman landowners from *Gallia Narbonensis* did he see the situation as having been altered.

Grenier (1945:216) points out the gaps in the evidence for such an hypothesis: how can one know the proclivities of the conquerors, so remote are they in time? It is possible that the parcelling of the land and the accommodation of the extant population varied from province to province. Fustel de Coulanges (1908) indicates that the Celts in the time of Caesar disposed of the land as if it were their own, but he does not establish the distinction between the owner of a private domain and the community member who regulated land use. In essence, we may be dealing with a system of use-rights, rather than outright ownership. The ownership might still have rested with the extended family or the community, despite Caesar's mention (*BG*, 6.13.5) of Druids settling inheritance and boundary questions. Caesar's comparison of the Celts with the Germans in this respect (*BG*, 6.21.1; 22.2.3) serves to point out the difference between the lands of pastoral nomads and those of agriculturists: the strict definition of boundaries. Probably some variety of true collectivism existed among the Germans, while the more agricultural Celts (who cultivated grapes, grains, pigs) moved in the direction of individual ownership. Much of the trend away from communal holdings would have come in two ways: from trade, and from the rise of craftsmanship, both of which will be discussed further.

Although the question of land tenure and the general status of the pleb in Celtic society is an important one, it is equally important to assess the toll that the Roman occupation of Gaul exacted on agricultural resources and, indirectly, on the agricultural population.

The effect of maurauding groups and siege tactics on commoners is unknown from the archaeological information, but Caesar's many comments about the need to forage farther and farther from the besieged city (e.g., Gergovia, Bourges, Alesia) to supply his army suggests an exhaustion of agricultural resources which may not have been immediately reparable. There is very little permanent damage which can be done to the land itself in such circumstances, although tools and other necessary farming equipment might be lost. The only real impairment of the agricultural potential of an area would probably be due to a decrease in population density. Plutarch says (Caesar 15) that Gallic casualties in the Gallic wars of 58-50 B.C. numbered one million, and that another million were taken captive. The same would be true in the case of maurauders, as with Caesar's armies: damage to the land would not be nearly as grave a threat as would be violence to commoners themselves. Yet if armies or maurauders intend to use an area for the same purpose repeatedly, a use-not-abuse policy would seem most feasible. This is not to suggest that there have not been uncountable times in history where whole populations have been laid to waste by vengeful raiding parties or occupying armies, but rural populations have a resilience undeniably lacking in urban populations whose wealth is expressed in possessions ripe for the torch.

Sex

Sex was a status-determining factor in Celtic society, although the treatment of women was generally more egalitarian than in many other groups on similar levels of social organization. Ammianus (XV.12) mentions Celtic women fighting alongside the men in battle; Tacitus (*Agricola,* 16) comments on the absence of sex distinctions among Celtic rulers; Diodorus Siculus wrote that Celtic women were not only like their men in their great stature, but were also their equals in courage (*Bibliotheke,* V, 28-31). There is a strong possibility that women served as Druids (see Chadwick, 1966:78-83). A rather enigmatic statement by Strabo (IV.5.3) stating that feminine roles in Gaul were the reverse of those in Rome might have been in reference to agricultural tasks and certain crafts (perhaps weaving?). It is the standard rhetorical antithesis, emphasizing the barbarity of the peoples on the periphery of the classical world. Caesar (6.19) mentions that Celtic husbands added an equal part of their own property to their wives' dowries, and that husbands and wives shared equal inheritance rights to their combined wealth. Men could take more than one wife (although the first wife held seniority) and had the power of life and death over their wives and children. Thus, the practice of polygamy and the basic Indo-European principle of patriarchal authority largely shaped the role of women despite more liberal practices in other areas.

Although the early Irish law tracts contain extensive information on the status of Celtic women in Christian Ireland, the information is of such late date (sixth-seventh century A.D.) as to be difficult to use. However, Binchy (1936) does make some careful suggestions. Women did not break ties with their own families on marriage, but continued to interact socially and politically with them. Rather than seeing this as the survival of a matriarchy, Binchy says it may actually be the beginning of natural kin recognition or cognatic rather than agnatic (through the male line) kin reckoning. There is apparently a parallel development in the evolution of Roman law (Binchy, 1936:186).

The Family

The family was the primary unit of Celtic society, patriarchal and strictly governed. The wives and children were continually under the husband's control; young men were emancipated from their father by vows of clientship; young women by marriage. The latter were raised by their mothers in most circumstances, but fosterage for both males and females may have been practiced. Generally Celts in Gaul were monogamous, but both polygamy and polyandry occurred. The nuclear family (parents and children) was part of the greater structure of the extended family, which in turn was part of the clan. Individual status was derived from these more complicated levels of organization, depending on how each individual functioned within the larger structures. There is good evidence that the clans functioned as a single political force. Grenier (1945:181) discusses the alliance of great families from city to city, sometimes effected by political reciprocity, sometimes by intermarriage. The successes of the Gaulish confederacy were due in great part to strong intertribal alliances, based ultimately on family connections.

Class, Status, and Political Organization

Grenier (1945:184) compares the level of Celtic social and political organization with that of the Age of Heroes in Homeric Greece, and suggests that the Celts were undergoing an evolution analogous to the beginnings of Greece and Rome. At the moment of conquest, the Celts were in the midst of a political transformation of some consequence, and had marked tendencies toward a constitutional government. Strabo (IV.4.3) recorded that they chose a chief magistrate annually, possibly meaning for all of Gaul. Caesar (*BG*, 6.13) confirms this:

> Of all these Druids one is chief, who has the highest authority among them. At his death, either any other that is pre-eminent in position succeeds, or if there be several of equal standing they strive for the primacy by the vote of the Druids, or sometimes even with armed force. These Druids, at a certain time of the year, meet within the borders of the Carnutes, whose territory is reckoned as the centre of all Gaul, and sit in conclave in a consecrated spot. Thither assemble from every side all that have disputes, and they obey the decisions and judgments of the Druids.
> (trans. H. J. Edwards)

However, it is not to be assumed that this transition was occurring without friction and strife. Tacitus (*Agricola,* 12), although speaking of Britain, describes the situation among the continental Celts:

> Originally the people were subject to kings; now they are distracted with parties and party spirit through the influence of the chieftains; nor indeed have we any weapon against the stranger races more effective than this, that they have no common purpose; rarely will two or three states confer to repulse a common danger, accordingly they fight individually and are collectively conquered.
> (trans. M. Hutton)

Yet tenuous and stormy as these intertribal relationships might have been, it is irrefutable that a strong tendency toward similar goals united them from time to time. It is most revealing that the Aedui, who fought in Caesar's ranks at the siege of Gergovia, joined the Gaulish resistance when Caesar retreated from that city. Caesar comments that not only all the cities, cantons, and sub-cantons, but also all families were divided into rival parties. These parties were represented by Aedui, who controlled the area roughly correlative with modern Burgundy, and the Sequani of Franche-Comté. These political rivals were the most powerful of the Celtic tribal groups. In the case of the Aeduan defection, Caesar saw its cause as the work of certain greedy, high-spirited youth:

> During these preliminary operations before Gergovia, Convictolitavis, the newly appointed Aeduan Vergobret, who had been bribed by the Arverni, opened negotiations with Litaviccus and his brothers, members of an aristocratic family and leaders of a gang of youths. He shared his bribe with them, and reminded them that they were free born men destined to rule. The Aedui alone, he explained, stood in the way of an otherwise certain Gallic victory: they alone kept other tribes loyal to Rome, who would have no chance in Gaul without them. He agreed that he was to some extent in my [Caesar's] debt, but argued that I had merely adjudicated on a cast-iron case, and that national liberty must be his first consideration.
> (*BG*, 6.37, trans. John Warrington)

The above is good indication that intertribal alliances were simply a continuation of familial and patron-client relationships on a larger scale: more powerful tribes bargained with lesser groups for allegiance and economic advantage. Doubtless, shifting fortunes brought rapidly changing political conditions, and the lack of cooperation among groups was due to differences in wealth, internal stability, and external pressure. What both Caesar and Tacitus observed were intertribal conflicts not unexpected in a situation of increasing socioeconomic stratification. It was certainly to Caesar's advantage to emphasize the disorganized character of Gaulish politics to his backers and to his detractors in the Senate, while at the same time underscoring the extensive danger to Rome of a few powerful Gauls; by doing so he could claim credit for his victories and note the capricious and isolated character of his defeats.

CONCLUSIONS

Classical sources mention only two classes in Celtic society: an aristocracy composed of Druids and knights, and the commoners. Within the aristocracy were certain status distinctions based on a combination of kinship, wealth, political influence, and occupation. The Druides were of the highest status, and served as moral philosophers and the embodiment of justice in the Celtic community; vates offered sacrifices and studied nature in an effort to presage, and were second only to Druides in status; bards composed and chanted hymns and were much esteemed in the community as a whole, although of less status than Druides or vates.

Discrepancies in the classical sources concerning the restrictions on the activities and occupations of Druids suggest that the role was a voluntary and flexible means of obtaining high status for individuals within the aristocracy. Becoming a Druid was apparently a matter of individual choice, based on personal abilities and predilections. Those members of the aristocracy who were not Druids were knights, and undoubtedly there was a status hierarchy among knights as well, probably based on kinship, wealth, and political influence. It is quite obvious that only exceptional individuals in the community (such as Dumnorix and Divitiacus) could fulfill the role of Druid while maintaining the kin, political, and economic contacts necessary for their roles as national leaders.

The other class mentioned by the classical sources was that of the commoner. There is little information on the occupations of this class of land-based agriculturalists, although Caesar implies that they were little more than serfs on lands owned by the aristocracy. Yet Caesar also noted the mutual advantages of clientship, which must be assumed to have been the major delineator of the relationship between the aristocracy and the commoners. Wolf (1966) points out that the client in patron-client relationships, unlike the landless serf in lord-serf relationships, has a significant amount of political importance to the patron, and especially so if he is a landholder (as may have been the case in Gaul). The client's allegiance cannot be possessed once and for all; instead, it is the result of a continuous effort on the part of the patron to gain the client's loyalty in exchange for protection. The need for protection, reflected in the fortifications of even the rudest settlements throughout Gaul, suggests that even commoners had a certain accumulation of wealth worth protecting. The rise to prominence in Gaul of such a system of reciprocity, both large- and small-scale, is, I believe, a result of competition for increasingly available wealth through trade with the classical world. The institution of clientage was the basis of Celtic political organization, from the level of the kin group to that of the Celts as a nation, and was a major factor contributing to the rise of the primitive state in Gaul.

PART II

THE ARCHAEOLOGICAL EVIDENCE

III

INTRODUCTION

THE archaeological evidence for social stratification among the Celts is varied and abundant. Unlike the literary data, in which problems of chronology and interpretation are encountered which are unlikely to be solved, the archaeological data are relatively straightforward, although problems of chronology still remain. Such data are of specialized use in this reconstruction of Celtic social structure, since only the spatial evidence of class distinctions is available for scrutiny. Without the archaeological evidence an entire class of Celtic society would have gone undetected, and perspective on the motivating factors in Celtic acculturation would have been lost.

The limits of this study have, to a certain extent, been set by the nature of the data. The sites to be examined, the time period chosen, and the types of evidence to be used as modes of comparison between sites were selected with the purpose of obtaining the greatest amount of data with the least possible ambiguity and qualification.

CHOICE OF SITES

All the sites discussed are of a single type: the *enceinte* or fortified enclosure. In France, these enclosures are of two predominant types: hill or promontory forts and low-lying or marsh-defended forts. The latter is less common, occurring among the Bellovaci and the Bituriges. All of these settlements were defended not only by their physical inaccessibility, but also by imposing defensive structures. Two major types of fortification were the *murus gallicus* (or Gaulish wall) and the Fécamp rampart. The murus gallicus has a framework of transverse and longitudinal timbers which are placed at varying intervals and are in some cases fastened by iron nails at their points of intersection. It has outer and sometimes inner dry-stone revetting walls; the outer walls are penetrated by

Key to Figure 4.

Site Number

North Coastal

1. *Camp d'Artus*, Huelgoat (Finistère)
2. *Kercaradec*, Penhars (Finistère)
3. *Le Châtellier*, Le Petit Celland (Manche)
4. *Camp du Canada*, Fécamp (Seine-Maritime)
5. *Câtelier*, Duclair (Seine-Maritime)
6. *Camp de la Ségourie*, Fief-Sauvin (Maine-et-Loire)
7. *Camp du Castellier*, Saint-Désir (Calvados)
8. *La Burette*, Banville (Calvados)
9. *Poulailler*, Landéan (Ille-et-Vilaine)

West Central

10. *Les Monts*, Neung-sur-Beuvron (Loir-et-Cher)
11. *Millançay*, Romorantin (Loir-et-Cher)
12. *Camp de César*, Sidialles (Cher)
13. *Camp de Chou*, Moulins-sur-Yèvre (Cher)
14. *Camp de César*, La Groutte (Cher)
15. *Les Fossés Sarrasins*, Châteaumeillant (Cher) MEDIOLANUM
16. *Avaricum*, Bourges (Cher)
17. *Camp de Châteloy*, Hérrison (Allier)
18. *Le Châtelier, les Pornins*, Luant (Indre)
19. *Camp de Cornouin*, Lussac-les-Châteaux (Vienne)
20. *Villejoubert*, St.-Denis-des-Murs (Haute-Vienne)
21. *Gergovia* (Puy-de-Dôme)
22. *Camp de Corny*, Meunet-Planches (Indre)

Southwestern

23. *Camp de Périgueux*, Coulounieix (Dordogne)
24. *Puy d'Issolu* (Lot)
25. *l'Impernal*, Luzech (Lot)
26. *Murcens*, Cras (Lot)
27. *Puy du Tour*, Monceaux (Corrèze)

South Coastal

28. *Ensérune*, Beziers (Hérault)
29. *Glanum*, Ste.-Remy-de-Provence (Bouches-du-Rhône)
30. *Entremont*, Aix-en-Provence (Bouches-du-Rhône)

Rhône-Saône Corridor

31. *Camp de Pommiers*, Soissons (Aisne)
32. *Le Châtelet*, Montigny-l'Engrain (Aisne)
33. *Le Câtelet*, Avesnelles (Nord)
34. *Mont Châtel*, Boviolles (Meuse)
35. *Vertault*, Laignes (Côte-d'Or)
36. *Mont Lassois*, Vix (Côte-d'Or)
37. *Mont Auxois*, Alise-Ste.-Reine (Côte-d'Or) ALESIA
38. *Bibracte* (Mont Beuvray), St. Leger-sous-Beuvray (Nièvre/Saône-et-Loire)
39. *Joeuvres*, St.-Maurice-sur-Loire (Loire)
40. *Le Châtelard de Chazi*, St.-Georges-de-Baroille (Loire)
41. *Essalois*, Chambles (Loire)
42. *Crêt Châtelard*, St.-Marcel-des-Félines (Loire)
43. *Ste.-Blandine*, Vienne (Isère)

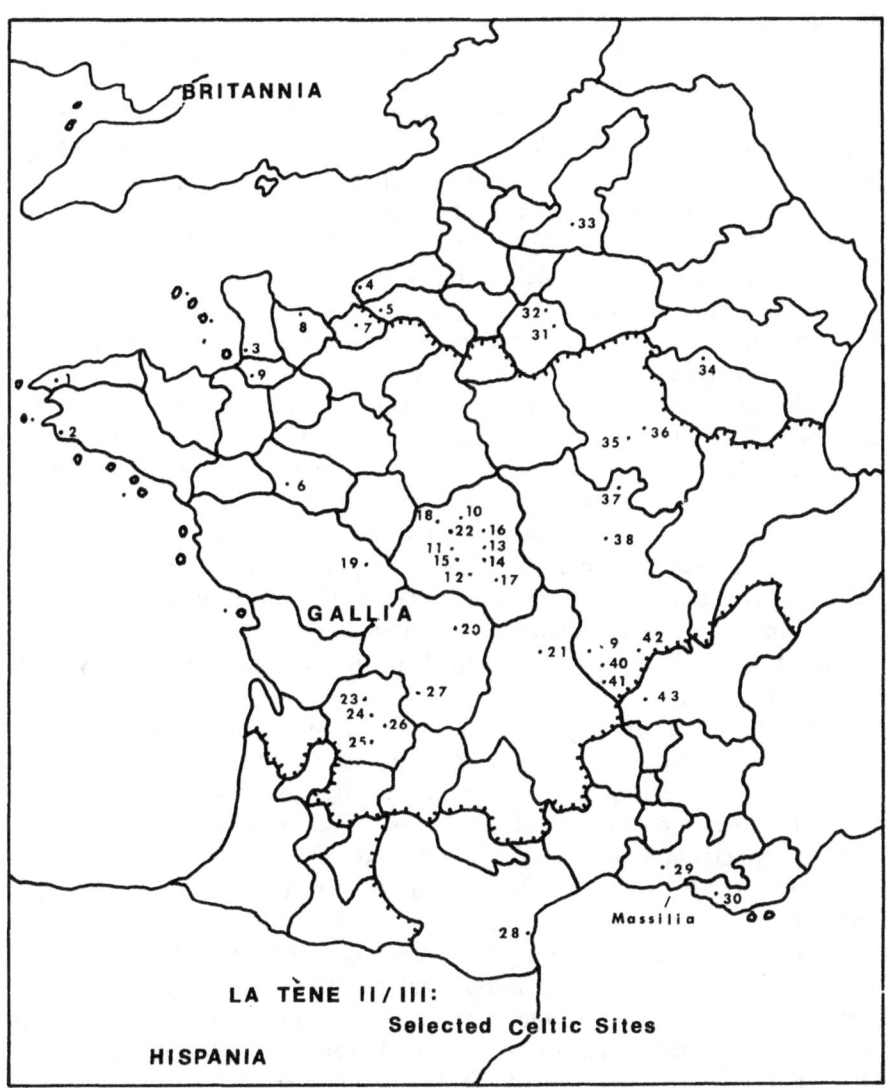

Fig. 4. Map of Archaeological Sites, La Tene II/III, Superimposed on the Outlines of Tribal Boundaries.

the projection of transverse timbers, and the interstices of this lattice are filled with rubble, stones, and earth. Not all muri gallici are located in France, but nails in such fortifications appear to be primarily a Gallic feature; in many German camps the timbers are mortised (an obvious exception is Manching in Bavaria, which is unmortised and employs nails). In his *Commentaries* (*BG*, 7.23) Caesar includes a description of the murus gallicus, which he admired so much that he had his troops duplicate it on occasion. The Fécamp rampart, or "high-dump" rampart, is of less intricate bank-and-ditch design, and contains no nails and as yet no evidence of timbers. The characteristics of the Fécamp rampart, according to Wheeler and Richardson (1957:11), are (1) a preference for commanding promontories which are cut off by a huge rampart, 20-30 feet high, and a broad, flat or bluntly rounded, canal-like ditch, with a steep external side sometimes reinforced by a small counterscarp bank, and (2) formidable entrances flanked by bold inturns of the main rampart.

The date for the muri gallici and Fécamp ramparts is La Tène III (mid-first century B.C.), with some possibility that a few examples of the former are late La Tène II (late second century B.C.). The most frequent location of muri gallici is in central Gaul; Fécamp ramparts are most common in the north. There is insufficient evidence to determine the relationship between the types, but two or perhaps three sites are reported (15, 17, and possibly 31) where Fécamp ramparts overlay muri gallici. I observed a similar relationship in the summer of 1973 at the oppidum of Levroux (Indre); an excavation report under the sponsorship of the Centre National de la Recherche Scientifique is in preparation by the director, Olivier Buchsenschutz.

No camps of either murus gallicus or Fécamp type are known to exist within the boundaries of Provincia Narbonensis, which may suggest that both muri gallici and Fécamp ramparts came into widespread use after 121 B.C. It should be noted, however, that timber does not seem to have been widely used within Provincia Narbonensis during the Iron Age.

Celtic hill forts were usually located near, or at the intersection of, rivers, occasionally near lakes or natural springs. Northern forts were often defended on at least one side by the sea. With some exceptions, most La Tène III sites examined are hilltop or mountaintop enceintes. The topography of France provides many opportunities for such a settlement system, particularly in the north, where limestone headlands afford easy modification, and in the region of the Massif Central, where dissection has left areas of notable relief. Few other types of Celtic settlement locations have been recognized, and it seems a safe assumption that the Celtic oppida were predominantly fortified hill-towns, occupied year-round in the more populated southern and eastern areas of Gaul, and periodically as a refuge in the sparsely settled north and west. In the latter areas, unfortified farm-villages most probably also existed, but surveys to date have not been directed toward identification of all extant settlement types.

Available modern excavation data are limited to a few dozen sites. There are certain types of evidence which, although varying widely in quality, may be extracted from the published reports and collated in a consistent fashion. In many cases, such as that of the important site of Bibracte, reports nearly 100 years old contain valuable information on Celtic urban settlement systems, industrial development in the Iron Age, and, ultimately, Gaulish social stratification. The effective use of earlier reports has easily doubled the sample size. Responsibility for the faithful translation of all site reports, except those sites in English excavated and published by Wheeler and Richardson (1957), lies solely with me.

Sites chosen for more detailed study are, as often as possible, those to which classical authors have referred, and for which there is geographic or literary confirmation of Celtic affiliation. This limits the extent of the area of unambiguous sites to the modern boundaries of France, which are essentially the same as those of Celtic Gaul.

CHRONOLOGY

The second Iron Age, or La Tène, has characteristically been described on the basis of observed changes in artifact types, burial practices, and art styles. Hatt (1970:101) has summarized the early work on La Tène chronology; he cites Tischler (1885) as the first to propose a chronology based primarily on the form of the fibula (a prototype of the modern safety pin used for securing garments). Tischler divided La Tène into three periods on the basis of a rough seriation of embellishments on the basic pin coupled with changes in sword length:

La Tène I—fibulae with gem-decorated foot; short swords
La Tène II—fibulae with ring or node; slightly longer swords
La Tène III—fibulae trapezoidal in shape; very long swords

The German archaeologist Reinecke, on the basis of funerary goods from sites in southern Germany, added to Tischler's formulation a period which was characterized by S-shaped fibulae decorated with birds or anthropoidal shapes and designated it La Tène A. Subsequent divisions were labelled B, C, and D. Hatt (1970:101-102) also mentions the Swiss savant Viollier, who systematically studied the necropoleis of the Swiss plateau to produce a chronology based on more precisely defined fibulae types. Viollier divided Tischler's La Tène I period into two periods: Ia was characterized in part by fibulae with a semi-circular arc. Viollier's Ia corresponded closely to Reinecke's La Tène A, which by comparative methods, was determined to have a fifth century B.C. date. Tischler (1900: 427) brought all the formulations together:

La Tène A = Ia   Type area: Rhine, Bavaria
                  Tumulus tombs, cremation, and inhumation
                  Hallstattian swords, fibulae

La Tène B = Ib   Type area: Marne cemeteries (northeastern France)
                  Inhumations under tumuli and in flat graves
                  Presence of coral used decoratively

La Tène C = II   Type area: La Tène (Switzerland)
                  Flat-graves, cremation
                  Presence of enamel used decoratively; lack of coral

La Tène D = III   Type area: Bibracte (France)
                  Cremation
                  Widespread use of enamel

In recent years, there has been a concomitant effort to date the periods and to relate them to changes in Celtic art styles. Hatt (1970:102) cites the work of Jacobsthal and others:

La Tène Ia	480-400 B.C.	"early Celtic style" flamboyant, inspired by Greek palmette
La Tène Ib	400-350 B.C.	"fantastic," from Scythian art
La Tène Ic	350-250 B.C.	"autonomous Celtic"
La Tène II	250-120 B.C.	"plastic" style
La Tène III	120-50 B.C.	"style of Entremont"

Rowlett (1968) has lately proposed certain changes based on his excavations of habitations and burials in Champagne:

La Tène Ia	480-400 B.C.	La Tène II	200-100 B.C.
La Tène Ib	400-300 B.C.	La Tène III	100 B.C. - A.D. 1
La Tène Ic	300-200 B.C.		

The difficulties encountered in comparing these various chronologies are considerable. Each period, if defined on the basis of stylistic changes, varies from one area of Europe to another and from one region of France to another. That variation has simply not been described for each region, and without consistently reliable data from many more sites in France than are presently available, a group of more accurate regional chronologies cannot be developed. However, in the course of this work, certain tentative regional differences in La Tène chronology have suggested themselves.

In isolated north coastal areas and also on the south coast where Mediterranean influences were considerably stronger than Celtic, Hallstattian ceramic types and design motives formed distinctive provincial complexes long after they had disappeared in most areas of central France. Sites such as le Camp du Canada (Fig. 4.4) and Kercaradec (2) in the north and Ensérune (28) on the southern coast exhibit "Ultimate Hallstatt" characteristics and date to the third century B.C. at Ensérune and the first century B.C. in the north.

After the Roman conquest (58-51 B.C.), the majority of northern sites were abandoned, while in the southern and central areas of France very little change is evident for at least another 50 years. Then, in response to Augustus' policy of moving the indigenous population from the heights to the valleys, Ensérune (28), Bibracte (38), Essalois (41), Crêt Châtelard (42), Joeuvres (39), Villejoubert (20), Murcens (26), l'Impernal (25), and le Camp de la Ségourie (6) were abandoned. Those sites which continued to be occupied well into the Gallo-Roman period also showed little evidence of immediately accelerated Romanization. Glanum (29), Ste. Blandine (43), Alesia (37), and Avaricum (16) are examples of sites which maintained cultural continuity through the last half of the first century B.C. Some were already extensively Hellenized, then Romanized (e.g., Glanum) and others remained distinctively Celtic (Alesia), but none showed much archaeological evidence of the conquest until the final years of the first century B.C. The chronologies of these sites are inextricably linked with documented historical events; yet, in instances other than outright destruction during the event, the archaeological assemblages reflect few changes for many years thereafter. This "culture lag" apparent in the archaeological data runs counter to the historical assumption that Roman acculturation continued apace in the last half of the first century B.C., and serves as a reminder that the most effective acculturation is economic and political, not military. The sites most affected by classical contacts were invariably the sites on major trade routes; the more important the route, the more quickly regional centers became Romanized. Late La Tène chronologies for the various regions of France must take the documented historical events of those regions into account to produce a valid account of their culture history, and to assess the cumulative effects of the Roman conquest on Gaul.

Rowlett (1968:129) suggests that by 200 B.C. the La Tène tradition had entered a period of slow decline, although the reasons for this are not well understood. Blacksmiths, in an attempt to improve metal-working techniques (and increase production?) by producing purer iron, actually diminished the quality of their weapons by removing carbon from the forging process, and thereby eliminated the means by which the Celts had unwittingly been producing steel. Polybius (2.33) notes the poor quality of Gallic swords in 225 B.C. In the south, Greek influence waned and Roman influence waxed, culminating in the formation of *Provincia Narbonensis* in 121 B.C. Roman traders engaged in more intensive trade into the interior than had the Greeks. They worked diligently to extend the demand for their goods far into the interior of Gaul; such indigenous sites as Bibracte served as distribution points for a trade network in existence, perhaps, since Neolithic times.

For the above reasons, the period between ca. 200 B.C. and A.D. 1 should yield the maximum amount of information on changes in Celtic material culture and, by extrapolation from that data, changes in Celtic social structure.

TYPES OF EVIDENCE

Some of the most readily obtainable data for La Tène II and III are geographical. The physical location, geographical description of the surrounding area, and the site layout are often the only types of data available for late La Tène settlements. Yet from that information, many inferences on population density, settlement systems, and site functions may be drawn.

Imported materials have been identified with some frequency, even in the earliest excavations. In fact, often only the imported ceramics were identified in the early reports, as indigenous pottery was thought to be of little interpretive use. Coins, both classical and Gaulish, were frequently reserved and studied, and allow us access to much information on commerce in Gaul.

Material for local use and for export has been recovered in the more extensive excavations. Much of it yields information on the various craft specializations in Gaulish society: bone-, wood-, and leather-working, ceramics, and metallurgy.

Burial data for the late La Tène period is the least useful source of evidence. The necropoleis are difficult to date closely enough to study contemporaneous grave lots. Bodies were generally cremated, so no demographic data are available except from sites in the south, where classical influences caused inhumation in tombs to be more popular. Even for those sites, no information has been published on the age and sex of individuals studied. Also, burial data offer the most tenuous information on social stratification when only the grave goods remain for study; there are simply too many unknowns.

The Geographical Setting

Monkhouse (1967:7) divides the pertinent geographical regions of modern France into Armorica (the north coastal region), Lowlands (of the north), Aquitaine (the southwest), Central Massif (the west-central area of the country), the Mediterranean Coast (south coastal), and finally the Rhône-Saône Corridor (Fig. 5). These differ somewhat from the regions delineated here, which were distinguished on the basis of archaeologically and ethnographically derived

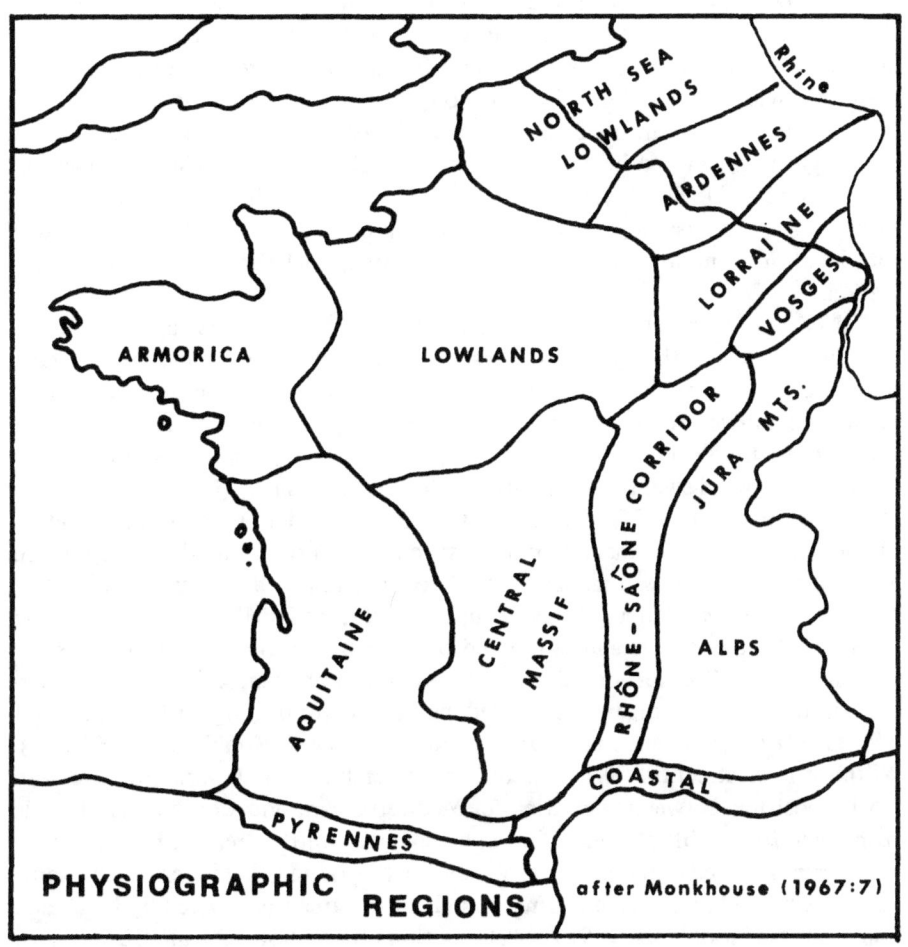

Fig. 5. Physiographic Regions of France.

information on settlement types, as well as on geographical distinctions (Fig. 6). The *north coastal* region (as used here) extends somewhat farther along the coast of the English Channel to the northeast, as far as the mouth of the Seine. The *west central* region is congruous with Monkhouse's Central Massif area, the *southwest* to his Aquitaine, and the *south coast* to his Mediterranean Coast. I have combined the Lowlands and Rhône-Saône Corridor regions of Monkhouse, despite obvious geographical diversity, on the basis of the use of the entire area as a route to the north: the British Isles, the North Sea Lowlands, and the Baltic. The regions as defined here are discrete culturally and, with a single exception (the Rhône-Saône Corridor), geographically, and each reflects a different dominant settlement system. All have yielded data on Celtic social structure through site location, function, and plan, as well as craft specialization and social stratification.

The *north coastal* region has great relief, both along its rugged coastline and inland, where the Hercynian (east) and Armorican (west) mountain ranges lie. Its climate is of the "western oceanic" type: there are strong on-shore winds along the far-western coast, and high humidity. The temperature is moderate throughout the year. In the interior uplands, however, conditions are far more bleak: raw, wind-swept and cloudy, with frost and snow (Monkhouse, 1967: 458). Approximately 75 percent of the region is under grassland, and modern Armorica is one of the main dairying districts in France. Along the coast, certain environments such as salt marshes afford arable land for the cultivation of grains.

The *west central* region is an upland area, bounded more or less by the thousand-foot contour, and composed of ancient granitic rocks. Known as the Massif Central, it covers one-sixth of the total area of France. The region is characterized by deep gorges and rugged pinnacles, contrasting with *peneplained* (flattened) areas of gentle undulations and flat surfaces (Monkhouse, 1967:524). Within the west central region there is considerable climatic variation, due both to its position between the Atlantic, Mediterranean, and Continental climatic zones and its variable altitude. The varied character of the areas within the region results in a mixed economy of sheep and cattle raising, fodder-crops and some grains. Until relatively recent times, much of the area was covered by beech and oak forests. Monkhouse (1967:432) mentions the remoteness and difficulty of communication of the area even today. Despite a limited geographical milieu, the craft specializations and iron and steel production that characterized the pre-conquest period are still among the economic assets of the Central Massif.

The *southwest*, termed the Basin of Aquitaine by Monkhouse (1967:313), is a triangular lowland comprising one-seventh of the area of modern France. It is characterized by gently rolling hills and valleys, and its soils are predominantly sand and clay. The major tributary in the region is the Garonne, which is navigable by boats of shallow draft almost to Toulouse. That city is situated at the western approach to the gap of Naurouze, or Carcassonne Gap, through which,

Fig. 6. Cultural-Geographic Regions of France.

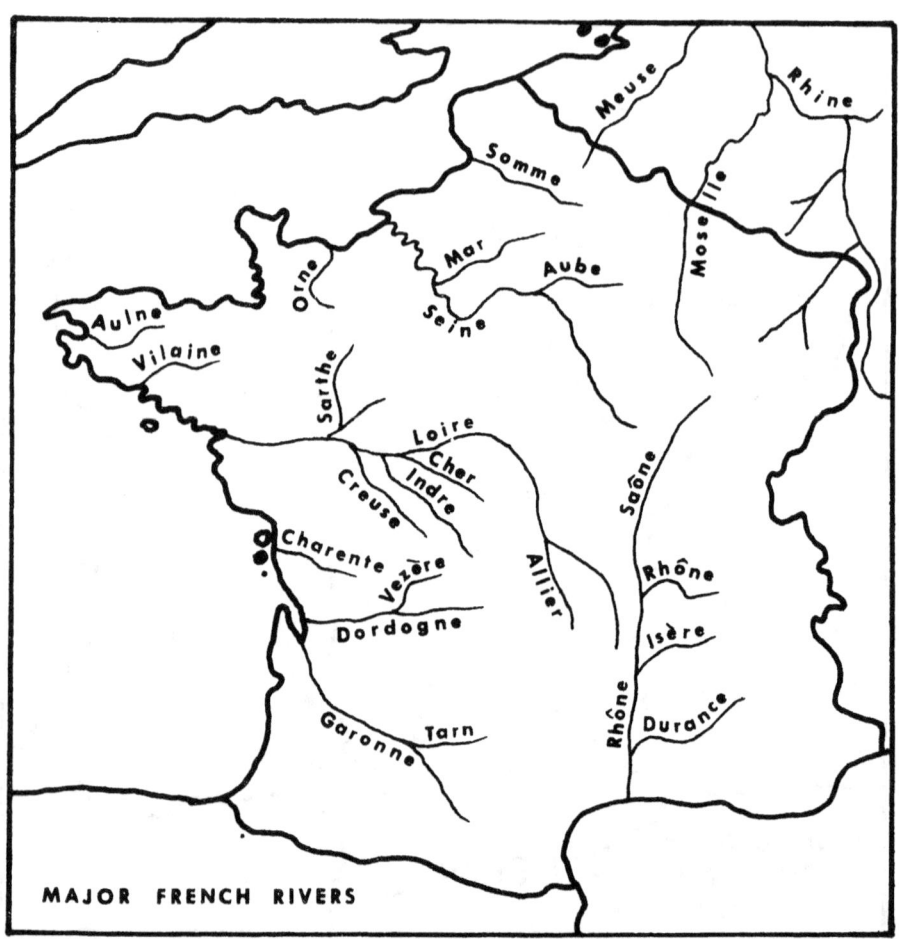

Fig. 7. Major French Rivers.

INTRODUCTION TO ARCHAEOLOGICAL EVIDENCE 41

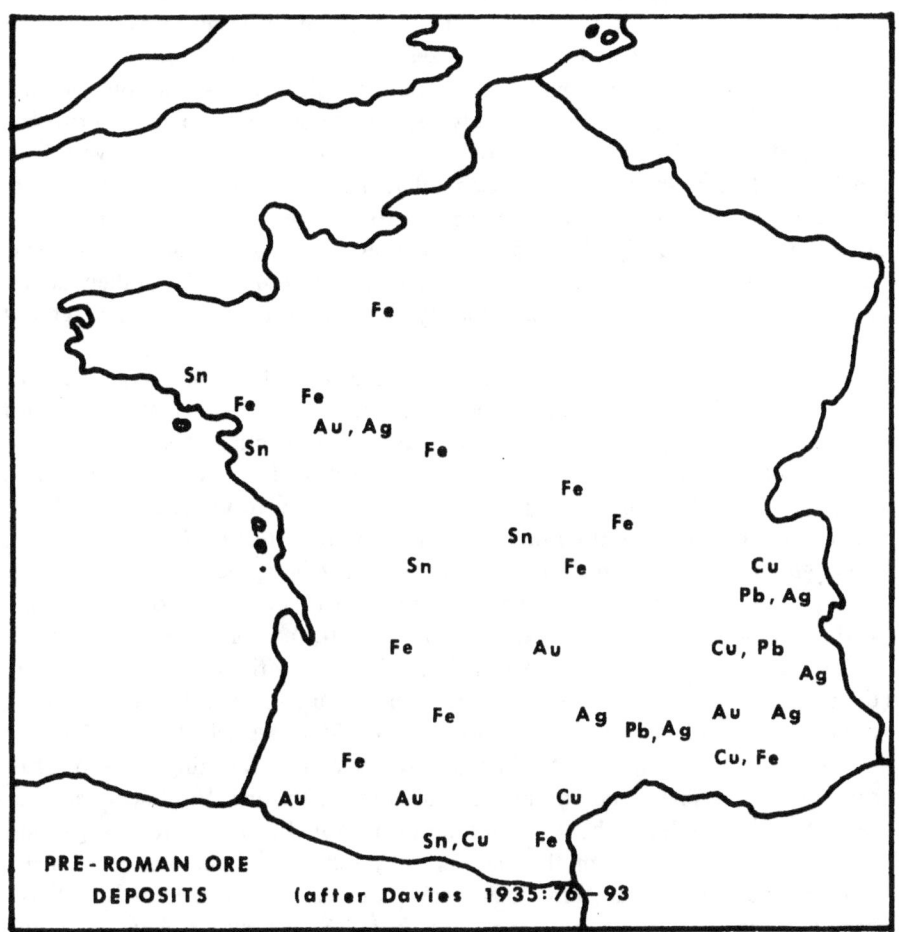

Fig. 8. Pre-Roman Ore Deposits.

for millennia, trade has passed between the Mediterranean and the Atlantic. The climate of the region is one of the most pleasant in France, an equability due to the proximity of the ocean and the Mediterranean Sea. The predominant agricultural products are grains and viticulture in the areas nearer the major watercourses, while the area to the south at the foothills of the Pyrenees is given more to transhumance: geese and turkeys, horses, pigs, and sheep.

The *south coastal* region is characterized by physical diversity but climatic similarities. Monkhouse (1967:402) divides the region into two areas: Provence to the east, from the Rhône River to the Alps, and Languedoc to the west from the Rhône to the Spanish border. Generally, the western area could be characterized as more heavily alluviated, while the eastern area owes its greater relief to the propensity of the Alps. The hot, dry Mediterranean climate unites these areas on the basis of vegetation, soils, and economic resources. For millennia the economy has been based on such typically Mediterranean crops as wheat, grapes and wine, and olives.

The *Rhône-Saône Corridor* region, as defined by Monkhouse (1967:366), refers only to the distinctive elongated feature referred to as "le couloir entre les montagnes," that is to say, only the constricted connecting valleys of the two rivers, bounded by the Alps and the Massif Central. For the purposes of this study, the definition of the region has been expanded to include the northern portion of the line of communication formed by the Rhône-Saône river system. Although this northern area has little in common geographically with the southern, there are and have been strong economic associations. The geography of the northern area presents two routes of easy access to the north coast: the Plateau de Langres, which gives access to the Paris Basin, and the Porte de Bourgogne (the Belfort Gap) between the Vosges and Jura mountains, which opens onto the Rhine. Faucher (1951-52, in Monkhouse, 1967:366) has called the region "un vestibule du Nord pour le Midi, du Midi pour le Nord," referring to its long history as a major line of communication in Western Europe. Vegetation and climate change completely between the cities of Montélimar (above Orange) and Vienne, moving north from the Mediterranean climate and complex of species to the northern European climatic and complex of species to the northern European climatic and vegetation zone. The Rhône-Saône river valleys are noted throughout the world for viticulture, the northern portion of the region for grains and dairying, the south for fruit and flowers.

The climate for the late La Tène period in France is thought, with minor exceptions, to have been similar to that of the present, and it is relatively safe to assume that land-use patterns for the two periods also bear some resemblance to one another. There are, of course, exceptions: viticulture moved steadily north after the conquest, as hardier varieties were developed. Increased deforestation through time also played an important part in changing patterns of land use in such areas as the west central region. Yet there are parts of modern France which continue to have communications problems due to topography, just as was the case in pre-conquest Gaul, or which continue to be sparsely populated, or which are as much in the mainstream of commerce today as they were 2,000 years ago.

IV

THE ARCHAEOLOGICAL EVIDENCE

THE uneven quality of the data from north coastal, west central, and southwestern areas makes extensive discussion of excavated sites unrewarding. The following section summarizes what is known about the settlement system, demography, economy, and social organization of the three areas; further information may be found in Appendix II. Subsequent sections will examine at length the data from the better-reported and more important south coastal and Rhône corridor areas.

NORTH COASTAL SITES

Settlement System, Demography, and Economy

The predominant settlement type in the north coastal area was that of the fortified camp or refuge, erected in times of emergency and occupied only under great stress. The area around most of the sites studied is poor agriculturally, although doubtless some farming was done. More likely the majority of the population relied on marine resources or, farther inland, animal and plant food, and only supplemented their diet with agricultural products. The large size of some of the enceintes indicates that they may have served to include domestic animals. Although there is no direct evidence for this area, it is likely that pastoralism was a way of life practiced by some.

The settlement system changed abruptly after the conquest, and the majority of sites were abandoned. Although the population density of this region seems to have been low before the conquest, the area appears to have suffered a major depopulation in response to, or as a result of, the Roman conquest, or that the population returned to simpler types of settlement typical of scattered farmers and herders. While some Gallo-Roman sites existed in the eastern part of the region, few Gallo-Roman sites or Roman roads are found in the west. The eastern group of north coastal sites completed the Rhône-Seine and Rhône-Calais trade routes to the sea and Britain, as important to the Romans as they had been to the Celts.

Social Organization

Social organization in the north coastal area would seem to have been the least complex in pre-Roman Gaul. The groups appear to have been scattered, perhaps transhumant, if one may interpret the absence of regional centers as an indication of low trade volume (compared with patterns established in the rest of Gaul). However, coins were minted, even by the distant and sea-oriented Osismii and Curiosolites, and some of these coins found their way to more southerly regional centers (see Fig. 11).

The data provide little real evidence on the level of organization of these people, but they were certainly organized enough to erect protective fortifications. We have no way of determining whether these were the work of one tribe or of many. That they were on a level of organization sophisticated enough to support chiefs capable of organizing and directing a large project seems assured. But we cannot estimate the importance of class distinction among these people except by ill-advised analogy.

WEST CENTRAL SITES

Settlement System, Demography, and Economy

West-central Celtic sites of La Tène III in France have, generally speaking, received somewhat less attention from excavators than is indicated from this study. This is due partially to the poor preservation of the smaller sites in heavily agricultural areas, where regular plowing and deforestation have taken their toll on the ramparts; it is more directly attributable to surveying difficulties in an area dominated by scrub woodland. The west-central sites were also slightly less important historically than those Rhône corridor sites to the west in the Rhône and Loire river valleys.

There are fortified camps and refuges (e.g., Sidialles) as in the north, but they are not as common. Regional trading centers, however, are more numerous —Avaricum (16), Villejoubert (?) (20), Puy du Tour (27)—and the areas they served, as measured by the distance between them, are noticeably smaller. There is still evidence of long-distance trade, but the shorter distances between these sites suggest a more active regional trade system than that witnessed in the north.

The physical location of sites is somewhat different as well: half of the sites discussed are low-lying, either in marshy areas or on slight rises between rivers or streams. All are nonetheless fortified, either by muri gallici or Fécamp ramparts, and two—Camp de César (12) and Les Fossés Sarrasins (15)—apparently have muri gallici over which Fécamp ramparts were constructed.

The low-lying character of the settlements of the Bituriges may have made them somewhat more attractive to the Romans after the conquest, as the subject populations were more easily controlled when they no longer commanded the heights of Gaul. This move toward relocation of the Celts had become provincial policy by the Augustan period. Although more pervasive Roman provincial policy was to leave regional economic patterns intact, in certain cases Roman interests were better served by concentrating the population around more easily governed centers. In some regions, equivalent autonomous centers which served Celtic purposes in times of independence duplicated Roman governmental functions and a percentage of such centers may have been abandoned. One would expect a certain amount of such reorganization (although no specific evidence for it exists) in moving from chiefdoms in the act of state-formation to a highly-organized governmental machine like the Roman Empire, despite Roman efforts to keep economic disruption at a minimum.

Social Organization

Caesar (*Commentaries,* 7) makes it quite clear that the center of Gaulish resistance was in the west, and that the urban centers of Gergovia and Avaricum were focal points of his campaign. The proximity of other sites of the same time period suggests high population density, an active trade network, and, by analogy, complex social stratification. Certainly artisans, agriculturalists, and the aristocracy existed in the active regional centers, not to mention a burgeoning class of merchants, petty officials, and retainers with abilities in civic administration to handle the civil services of such cities. To deny that these individuals were present and active in Celtic urban life at the time of the conquest is to suggest that cities of 40,000 run themselves. To assert that these individuals were primarily colonials, as Caesar implies, is to make the fallacious assumption that, before the conquest, the Celts were willing to have outsiders run their cities for them and harvest all the profits of trade agreements with the classical world. Even after the conquest, it was Rome's policy to allow the cities self-governance.

SOUTHWESTERN SITES

Settlement System, Demography, and Economy

The provinces of Guyenne and Gascogne deserve separate treatment on the basis of literary evidence (Strabo, *Geographia,* IV), geographic distinctions, and the paucity of archaeological data. Although the area promises a great deal of information on the major land trade route between the Mediterranean and the Atlantic, the Aquitanian Way, little excavation of late La Tène period sites has taken place.

With a sample of only five sites, it is difficult to make any general remarks about the predominant settlement type or the population density of the southwestern region of Gaul. Yet it is apparent that at least three of the sites—Murcens (26), Puy du Tour (27), and Puy d'Issolu (24)—were regional centers of trade with active industrial quarters. Such sites probably owed their regional prominence to their location on the so-called Aquitanian Way, the southern trade route to the Atlantic, between Lyon and Bordeaux. Moreau de Jonnes (1851: 604) cites Caesar on the population of Aquitania at the time of the conquest (fewer than 251,340) and comments that the low population figure explains Aquitania's lack of involvement in the move toward Gaulish independence. Insufficient survey of the area to date does not permit a similar conclusion about the population density from the archaeological evidence.

Social Organization

Somewhat more information on Celtic social organization is available from southwestern sites than from those in the north, but it is still rather unsatisfactory. Craft specialization obviously existed, and both industrial and agricultural vocations were possible. Grenier (1945:180) states that Uxellodunum had a master, who supported numbers of specialists by the system of clientage, and the excavation of Puy d'Issolu substantiates the speculation that numerous specialists did indeed labor within its ramparts. We know that at least two and, by inference, three classes existed in the southwestern area of France in La Tène III: artisans, agriculturalists, and an aristocracy which governed the politics and the economy of the regional centers.

SOUTH COASTAL SITES

South coastal Celtic sites in France have a peculiar history of their own. They came under strong Mediterranean influence (especially Greek), giving Gaul initial direct contact with the classical world and, simultaneously, they were peripheral to the Celtic world, lagging noticeably behind the rest of Gaul for most of the Iron Age. Because of their classical affinities, many of the sites in the area which became Provincia Narbonensis have been carefully excavated. We shall discuss three sites containing La Tène III horizons which reflect these mixed, and often opposed, influences.

Ensérune

The oppidum of Ensérune (28) is situated in the western section of the department of Hérault, about 9 km southwest of Béziers, near the national route between Béziers and Narbonne. It is located on a barren spur of clay and Pliocene conglomerates which emerges from the coastal plain stretching between the rivers Orb and Aude to the south and the first foothills of the Cevennes and the sea to the north and east. It is 120 meters above the plain, with the point of the spur facing east. Its general aspect is of an elongated hill, enlarged and higher toward the west and at the same time sinking progressively elsewhere, except on the south, where the terraces have abrupt slopes. The hill is crowned by a triangular plateau of 37 acres. A natural break in the geological strata divides the point or acropolis on the east from the spacious, gently inclined plateau of the hill's western limits.

Ensérune was first explored in 1843 by the Abbé A. Geniesis, and then in 1915 by an amateur, F. Mouret. The site was extensively excavated by Jean Jannoray beginning in 1945, and his report was published in 1955 in *Bibliothèque des Ecoles Françaises d'Athènes et de Rome*, vol. 181. The following summary of findings relies heavily on Jannoray's excellent site report.

In the oldest occupation at the end of the first Iron Age, the summit and the edges of the plateau were levelled and huts and hollow silos built out of the rock (Fig. 9). Later, in La Tène I, new construction in stone appeared on a series of man-made terraces. The promontory offered much to human groups seeking refuge: a position in itself heavily fortified, it had defenses of steep cliff and the approaches were covered on the southwest and northwest by two points at the foot of the hill, almost like a natural moat. The possession of this refuge assured the control of the flat country to those who held it. Agricultural production of the fertile plain and the fishing resources of the two ponds (now dessicated) provided ample subsistence. The lack of water on the hill posed a difficulty which was overcome by the excavation of cisterns into the underlying tufa. Physically, Ensérune is situated between mountain and sea on an important trade route into the interior; the nearby Mediterranean shore provides good anchorages. The oppidum was an indigenous emporium and fortification in a rural environment, and yet open to the effects of civilization. These factors produced a complex habitation of essentially Mediterranean type, with both indigenous and external influences evident for all periods.

There were three major periods of occupation at Ensérune:

I. 560/550–430/420 B.C.
II. Stratum I: 425–375 B.C.; Stratum II: 375–280 B.C.
   (La Tène I and II)
III. Stratum I: 280–225 B.C.; Stratum II: 225 B.C.–A.D. 25.

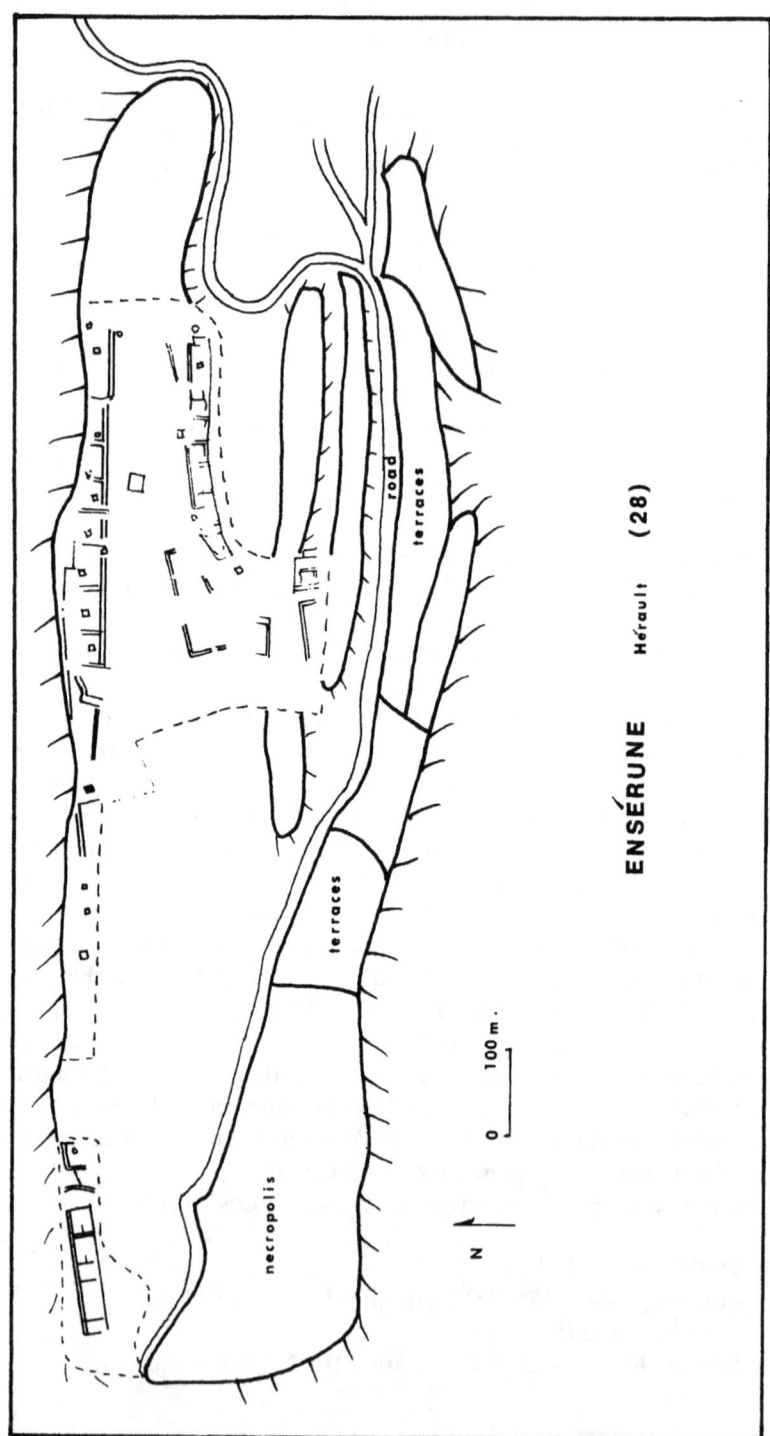

Fig. 9. Plan of Excavations, Ensérune (28) Herault.

THE ARCHAEOLOGICAL EVIDENCE 51

The first period of occupation yielded strata containing animal bones, charcoal, marine shells, ceramics and huts, and has been dated by Jannoray from the end of the first Iron Age, before La Tène. The village was on the western extremity of the plateau; hut floors were found scattered or two by two. Silos served as storage; no dolia (storage vessels used to transport wine and oil) were recovered. Jannoray considers this a most primitive aspect, although silos are common at this time period throughout the Mediterranean. Metal materials were rare, and limited to a few ornaments; the lithic assemblage consisted of characteristic Neolithic polished axes and grinders, bone combs (possibly to card wool?), and indigenous ceramics. The latter were badly fired and poorly tempered, with incised decorations and cord or finger impressions. The best representative form is pressed down from deep basin, carinated or pot-bellied, with a handle thickened in the form of a flange.

The second period of occupation is represented by two strata. The lower stratum is poor in ceramic finds, but what sherds were recovered were of the Ionian painted tradition. Attic black-figured wares and the grey pottery of the west were also recovered. The use-area of the site is slightly wider than in the previous period, suggesting increased population. The upper stratum is distinguished by some rearrangement and levelling of the north and south slopes. It is rich in ceramics, baked clay objects, and metal. It yielded the oldest stone constructions of the oppidum in the form of dwellings. The natural slopes were further terraced and houses built upon them. These dwellings were rectangular and aligned north-south along the terraces. Among the ceramics were red-figured wares dating from the last quarter of the fifth century and the beginning of the fourth century. At the top of the stratum were found Attic (from an area in Greece including Athens) and Campanian (an area of Italy near modern Naples) craters or bowls of the late fourth century. Poorly made dolia were recovered throughout the strata of Period II, as were grinding apparatus. From the nature of the artifacts, the date of the lower stratum of Period II is 425-375 B.C. (La Tène I) and the upper, 375-280 B.C. (La Tène II).

The first enclosure of the hilltop occurred in Period II. A powerful polygonal wall, relatively well preserved on the north but destroyed on the south by additions to the habitation, girded the plateau. The fortifications were of an indigenous, not Hellenic, style. Two funerary levels in the necropolis area of the site (which was outside the fortifications) correspond to Period I.

The third period of occupation, immediately beneath the plow zone, also contained two strata. They yielded an extensive city-plan from the area of the plateau. The basic plan was an elongated checkerboard, with the major axis corresponding to that of the hill. The lower stratum is not temporally separated from previous and later levels; it resembles both. The upper stratum, through the presence of characteristic dolia, yields evidence of exchange with Magna Graecia (through Marseille); there are also imitations of Italic ceramic models introduced by Roman colonials in meridional Gaul.

Italiote pottery, present in Period II, is abundant in Period III. Also present are various wares for ordinary use from the workshops of Magna Graecia (which benefited at this time from the Athenian eclipse) which were diffused throughout the western Mediterranean. The lower portions of the upper stratum yielded Campanian wares, while the final top centimeters produced characteristically Roman ceramics. The lower stratum may be interpreted as representing economic exchange with the Greek world and Campanian workshops, and with the provinces of Iberia nearby. The upper stratum is dominated by such imports from Roman Italy as ceramics, and the presence of Roman coinage as well underscores the importance at this time of trade with Rome. The metalwork in both strata of Period III is indigenous in style and execution and emphasizes the importance, despite outside influences, of this indigenous Gallic industry.

The area of the necropolis yielded four major periods of use:

I. Urnfield (food offerings): 1st Iron Age, 650(?)-600 B.C.
II. Circular shafts (no food offerings):
    a. 550-425 B.C.
    b. 425-375 B.C.
    c. 375-325 B.C.
III. Circular shafts (food offerings): 325-250 B.C.
IV. Tombs (food offerings): 225 B.C.-A.D. 1.

In the quarter of habitation, another internal distinction may be made on the basis of artifacts and construction details. The first subdivision is 225-100 B.C., the second 100 B.C.-A.D. 25 in Period III, with a destruction level between.

One of the most important single artifact types at Ensérune is the dolium. There are two major types in Period III: type one is carinated, Hellenic inspired, and dates to 225-110 B.C.; type two is spherical, Italic inspired, and belongs to the final occupation of the site—100 B.C.-A.D. 10/20. One recovered dolium (dating between 225-200 B.C.) is of particular interest. It depicts on its side a nude female figure holding grapes in her right hand and a scepter or baton in her left. Jannoray says that although grossly done it most certainly is a bad transposition of elements of Greek Dionysian symbolism. Dolia were sometimes marked with bunches of grapes or sheaves of grain to indicate their contents, and were inscribed with Iberian characters. The latter particularly point to the indigenous origin of these dolium types, since the language of Ensérune was Iberian; the Pyrenees imposed no cultural barrier. The millstone found at Ensérune is of regional origin as well.

The changes and progress noted in Jannoray's detailed artifact studies do not seem to be accompanied by economic revolution. There is a permanence of fashions of building (reflecting a way of life), although they grow more Roman. The forms of existence and of the economy did not cease to be those of a rural population which drew its resources from the plain surrounding the oppidum. The modest riches of grain and wine furnished Ensérune with an exchange currency for commercial relations with nearby regions or countries. The permanence of ancient and native modes of life is marked in every period.

The necropolis adds somewhat to the picture: Jannoray felt that the military organization represented was aristocratic and the social organization feudal, based on the distribution in the burials of arms and objects of adornment and, in some cases, horses. He also felt that one group of burials, rather than representing indigenous ruling minority, instead were Celtic invaders of the last quarter of the third century who settled among the indigenous peoples of Ensérune. The sweep of Gallic bands across the Mediterranean was a matter of record from the end of the third century. Important periods of transformation at Ensérune occurred around 425 B.C. and 225 B.C.

Let us more carefully observe the major influences operating on Ensérune, following Jannoray's formulation.

The Greek World. An indigenous culture at the end of the first Iron Age could reasonably be expected not to change at the precise moment when history records Hellenic expansion. Excavation reveals Attic wares, but the assumption is often made that after the founding of Massilia Gaul was fastened permanently to the Greek world. Of primary importance, of course, was the founding of Marseille in about 600 B.C. Yet as great as Greek influence was, Ensérune was apparently nothing more than an indigenous site open to the economic penetration of the Greek world. For sites in the area of Marseille a Gallo-Iberic character was gradually replaced by Gallo-Greek. Marseille profited by the decline of other countries' economic interests in the area, and by the Phocean (an Ionian colony in Asia Minor) regression in Spain. This led to increased activity of groups of Hellenistic culture in the area from the Alps to the Ebro, a river which flows from central Spain to the Mediterranean. From the eighth and seventh centuries, Hellenism had begun to expand around the borders of the western basin of the Mediterranean. South Italy and Sicily were the first steps of a colonization movement which made these regions a new Greece of the west. Herodotus (IV, 152) mentions the importance of the western Mediterranean to the tin trade, as does Diodorus (V, 38, 5). Tin from Brittany brought through the Narbonne region was the greatest market item of the Celts.

The league of the Carthaginians and the Etruscans cut off Athenian trade for two generations, from about 490 to 425 B.C., during which time Marseille fell into obscurity. The Greeks were evicted from Gaul and Spain, and Marseille was practically isolated. After 425 B.C. the Mediterranean imports were again Attic, until about 330 B.C., when Ensérune began to import from south Italy.

Rome, with Marseille's help, ameliorated Marseille's position by besting Carthage (202 B.C.) and opening up the Spanish Levant. Marseille actually had a rather tenuous position: Massiliote merchants were preoccupied with economic penetration, and were not interested in acquiring territory. The economic activity of Marseille was responsible for the diffusion of Hellenism in south Gaul.

Hellenic contributions to Ensérune are in evidence. The architecture of Period II, while not the work of Greek colonists, is Greek-inspired, but closer in type to coastal Iberian oppida. The town was not a Greek post, as even superficial comparison with such Greek-founded cities as Glanum will attest. The Greek ceramics are all present through exchange; none are made locally. The percentages of indigenously Greek ceramics rise and fall according to the economic fortunes of Marseille.

Greek as well as indigenous money was in use, although the coinage of Magna Graecia is absent despite the presence of its ceramics; this was probably due to a Massiliote policy which encouraged the use of indigenous coinage. Coins from Greek and Romanized cities along the Spanish coast and the Gulf of Lyon reflect the existence of some internal trade. Greek merchants were always eager to use local coinage to inspire confidence among the Gauls that the indigenous inhabitants were involved in the area's economic affairs, and Jannoray's list of recovered coins would seem to bear this out. Linguistically, the use of Greek at Ensérune was limited and began no earlier than the second century B.C. This is true not only at Ensérune but also around the Gulf of Lyon and the provincial hinterland of Marseille. The use of Greek was probably limited to the commercial domain which would explain the long absence in Hellenic texts of indigenous epigraphy. This late Greek influence in Gaul, after so many years of only superficial acculturation, was due to the extension of Roman protection to Marseille in 118 B.C.

The Celtic World. Celtic imported materials at Ensérune consist of a few bronze fibulae; the volume of exchange suggests trade with the Hellenic world was most important. The poverty of the first Iron Age at Ensérune suggests that it was on the periphery of Iron Age I development, and even at the periphery of the entire Languedoc-Roussillon area. Apparently two bands of invaders traversed southwest Europe in the first Iron Age, but their origins and chronology have not been well established. The first group was from the mountainous Jura region, arriving by the Saône and Rhône rivers. The second group came over the Swiss plateau by way of Savoy and the valley of the Isère, and down the Rhône. It was out of this first Iron Age milieu that the culture of the group initially populating Ensérune was produced.

The second Iron Age (La Tène I and II—Period II) culture at Ensérune was Iberian, like that of the Languedoc-Mediterranean-Roussillon area generally. There was, however, a prolonged Hallstattian influence in the region, as witnessed by fibulae types. In the third occupation of the oppidum, Gaulish coinage in Greek characters appears in great quantity. Dress and equipment are a vulgate of the La Tène modes. Ceramics are forms preferred in the two periods before La Tène. Current La Tène III ceramic production is exactly analogous to that of Bibracte. Stelae fragments from a nearby site (Cayla de Mailhac) suggest continued local popularity of the severed head cult. Still Ensérune was obviously a Gaulish center at the point of Roman intervention.

The Iberian World. One of the major Iberian contributions to the culture of Ensérune was metalworking, beginning in Period II of its occupation. Iberian ceramics were also common. Perhaps most interesting is the linguistic evidence. The alphabet used in Period II at Ensérune is identical to the alphabet in use on the Mediterranean coast of Spain. Iberian coinage appears in the second century (ca. 175 B.C.) until ca. 70 B.C. The Roman intervention began in 118 B.C., but the continued presence of Iberian symbols and inscriptions is proof of the permanence of ancestral forms at Ensérune and in the surrounding area. Graffiti are in the same alphabet and idiom as that of the Mediterranean coast of Spain. Beginning in the first quarter of the fourth century, some ceramics from Ensérune bear the Spanish rectangular cartouches as maker's marks. There are no Greek or Latin documents from Ensérune. The language in use there exactly parallels that of the Spanish Levant and Catalonia.

The Roman World. Ensérune did not suffer the bloody struggle with Rome as did the Saluvian city of Entremont on the west side of the Rhône. The indigenous peoples conserved their modes of life and continued to inhabit their ancient oppidum. Beginning with Calvinus' victory over the Saluvii in 123-22 B.C., the Languedoc-Mediterranean-Roussillon area was subjected in earnest to Roman dominance. The castellum of Aquae Sextiae guarded their interests. The menace of the coalition of the Allobroges and the Arverni caused Rome to annex the area west of the Rhône in 121 B.C. While the Greeks had participated in the indigenous economy, the Romans confiscated it. After 121 B.C., the region was in economic and political subjection to Rome. Adding to the burden of the indigenous peoples of the area was the invasion of the Cimbri in 110 B.C., which accounts for a destruction level between Periods II and III. The progress of Romanization led to the spontaneous extinction of indigenous money, as it led to the later abandonment of the oppidum. There are a few indigenous coins with Latin characters and legend. In architecture, Roman influence was perhaps most noticeable. Cement, a new building material, was used for the first time in Period III. Masonry, paving plaster types, painted stuccos, and hypocausts were all signs of urbanism, yet apparently the builders were still indigenous. The oppidum was aggrandized and embellished, but not transformed into a Roman city. The occupants were not Italiote, as at Glanum. In ceramics, there were

Roman imported wares which had contained olives, oil, and wine, all new to the indigenous peoples. In sum, it was not until the Roman occupation of the Languedoc-Mediterranean-Roussillon area that indigenous modes were broken down and replaced. Until that time, and for a surprising period of time after the Roman conquest, the area retained its indigenous quality.

Glanum

The ancient city of Glanum (29) is situated near the small modern town of St-Rémy-de-Provence (Bouches-du-Rhône), near Avignon and Njmes, in the delta of the river Rhône. Glanum was mentioned by Pliny (*Nat. Hist.*, 111, IV, 5); Ptolemy recorded its geographical coordinates and identified Glanum as being situated in the country of the Saluvii (*Geogr.* II, X).

Glanum was also on the Via Domitia, the continental route between Spain and Italy by way of Geneva, a route which was used both in Roman and pre-Roman times. Glanum was excavated by Henri Rolland, beginning in 1945, and the results have been extensively published in *Gallia*. The following discussion is based on Rolland's findings. The site was inhabited first in the Chalcolithic period. In the early levels, fifth century Massiliote monies, fragments of indigenous urns and sherds of Greek vases appeared: Ionian, Phocean (from Ionian Phocaea on coast of Asia Minor) and Attic black-figured wares. Glanum became a Greek colony at the end of the third century B.C., unlike Ensérune and Entremont, which never quite lost their indigenous status. In 96 B.C. the buildings of Glanum were in part razed; in 49 B.C., with the fall of Marseille, Greek Glanon became Roman Glanum. The habitation of Glanum was finally terminated by the German invasions of A.D. 270.

The occupation sequence is as follows:

Glanum I (Hellenistic period): 100 B.C.
Glanum II (Greco-Roman): 100 B.C. to ca. 40 B.C.
Glanum III (Roman): 49 B.C. (Augustan) to A.D. 300.

The extensive stone architecture of both private and public buildings at Glanum attests to active use of the nearby quarry-site throughout the occupation of the city. The public baths at Glanum date to Period II; there are also porticoes and atria and numerous other architectural characteristics we attribute to the Graeco-Roman world.

Glanum is an excellent example of the role of Marseille as a civilizer in the western Mediterranean. The city plan of Glanum, as well as the techniques of architecture for Glanum I and II, leave little doubt that Greeks, and not acculturated indigenous peoples, occupied the city. Romanization began in the area with the foundation of Aix (123 B.C.) and was intensified by the stay of the legions of Marius (104-102 B.C.). The fall of Marseille at the hands of Caesar (49 B.C.) ended Greek influence entirely, but habitation of the city continued until the period of the barbarian invasions.

Entremont

The site of Entremont (30) is located 3 km north-northwest of Aix-en-Provence (Bouches-du-Rhône). To the north is the rich plain of the Durance and the way to Italy; to the south is the lake of Berre. The oppidum is on a plateau 365 m above sea level, and triangular in form. The site has been excavated and its description published by Ferdinand Benoit (1957), and this summary essentially follows Benoit's findings.

During the period of Gaulish independence (4th-2nd century B.C.) Entremont was the capital of the Celto-Ligurian confederation of the Saluvii. The city was an obstacle to the expansion of both the Massiliote merchants and the Roman armies. In 123 B.C. Entremont was assaulted and captured, and the city destroyed. In 122 B.C., Sextus Calvinus founded nearby Aix (Aquae Sextiae Salluviorum), the first Roman city in Gaul.

Before the introduction of these strong pressures for Romanization, Entremont had been an active and prosperous Greco-Gaulish city. Termed a *polis* by Diodorus Siculus, it occupied a flat escarpment somewhat greater than 7.5 acres in area. The city plan (Fig. 10) is very different from the usual Celtic agglomerations built merely for the purpose of the hunt or war; instead, it evokes the cities of Greece, Magna Graecia, and Etruria. These cities (architecturally speaking) subordinate individual fantasies under law, and are obedient to the demands of hygiene and security, traffic, and religious precepts. Such cities are the product of a conception of a whole which gives organization to architecture: there are large wide streets, rectangular blocks, and yet the houses are often curvilinear and delimited by wheel-ruts. Conditions of habitation were relatively primitive: There are one-room houses (rarely two-room) and no pleasant apartments adjacent to central courts, as at Glanum. Grain was contained in cylindrical silos made of wood with stone covers. Dolia and amphoras for water and wine were used, the latter being imported from Marseille.

Entremont would seem to be the first example of urbanization in Gaul (except for the Greek city of Marseille). Within its gates were groups representing all the arts and trades. Entremont was also a center for tribal stores; its functions for the Saluvii were both agricultural and industrial.

The counterpoise of an oil-press and flagstones with circular grooves are witness to oil-making installations not unlike those of Roman design. Grain was prepared on a rectangular quern with lateral grooves (a Greek type); after the La Tène II period, circular querns appeared.

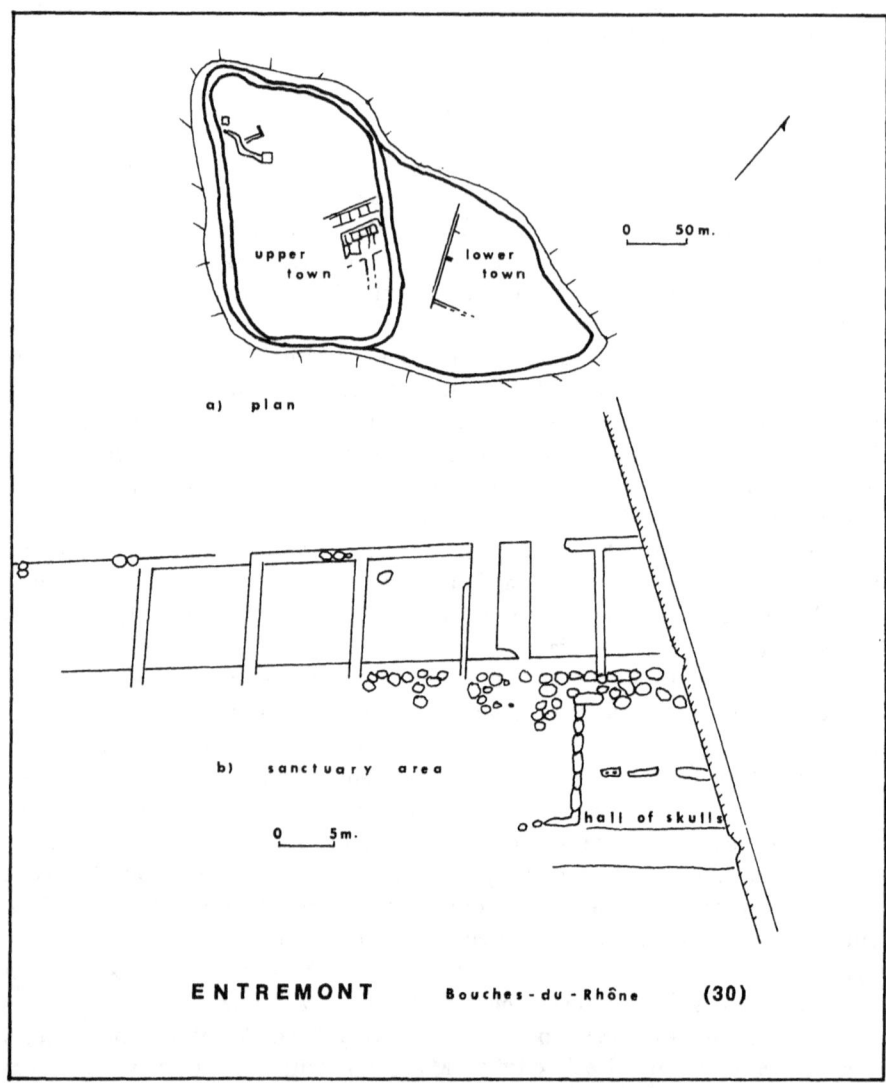

Fig. 10. Plan of Excavation, Entremont (Aix-en-Provence) Bouches-du-Rhône.

A number of ironworks, agricultural and industrial, indicate the development of edge tool making; digging picks, anvils, sickles, scissors, iron pincers, and stone-cutting mattocks were recovered in this area. The inhabitants of Entremont worked in gold and bronze as well as iron. In leather, fragments of helmets, doublets, and breastplates were recovered. Pendants of polished coral, indicative of commerce with Marseille, are in a mode which spread up the Rhône valley at the end of the Hallstatt epoch. Great jars were recovered marked with pentagrams; firing ovens occupied a quarter in the upper city. Most of the coinage recovered represents that of the Greeks of about 200 B.C. Two major hoards were found, one of 435 pieces, one of 100 pieces. Also recovered was the money of the Allobroges and Rome, both dating from the first half of the second century B.C.

Thus occupation by force of arms was preceded by certain humanistic exchanges, which attest to the importance of commerce with Marseille: jewels or coral and bracelets of glass and amphoras holding the wines of Rhodes and Campania and Campanian vases all bear witness to the abundant exportation which made the Italo-Greek merchants of the second century B.C. wealthy. A more tangible example of the interaction between indigenous and external elements is statuary that represents important aspects of the indigenous culture, but was executed in a style which reveals knowledge of Graeco-Etruscan plastic arts and three-dimensional sculpture.

The area called the Sanctuary is one of the most important parts of the site. Recovered votive objects in an evolved in-the-round style represent aspects of the distinctively Celtic severed-head cult. The trophy skull is the veritable god of these sanctuaries. A sacred way to the sanctuary, lined with mosaics, climbs the flank of the enceinte northwest of the acropolis. The sanctuary itself is constructed on the highest part of the city. A great hall five meters wide and of unknown length was apparently of great religious importance. The sanctuary itself, reminiscent of sanctuaries found at Roquepertuse, Glanum, Castelveyre de Sainte-Blaise, and Cadenet, has niches for severed heads. A fragment of the lintel from Entremont dates to before 123 B.C. Human skulls of individuals between 30 and 50 years old, bearing traces of suspension or trephination, were recovered. The excavation revealed the violent destruction of cult objects and a paving-over of the area at the time of the Roman occupation.

Entremont has not the consistently Gaulish flavor of the occupations at Ensérune, but neither does it appear to have been an outpost of Greek colonials, as was Glanum. The three sites offer, within roughly the same area, three separate accommodations to the presence of external cultures.

Settlement System, Demography, and Economy

The predominant settlement type of the south coastal sites is the same as that of the rest of Gaul, the enceinte or hill-fort. However, functional distinctions and historical events have given these sites a unique dimension: direct and long-standing contact with the classical world. Because of this association, more Provençal sites have been excavated, and the reports for south coastal Celtic sites are more complete. The three sites discussed above—Ensérune, Glanum, and Entremont—reflect varying degrees of acculturation. Ensérune was influenced in turn by trade with the Iberians to the south along the Costa Brava; by Greeks, who by establishing the free port of Marseille, exerted influence by example and economics; and finally by the Romans, who held sway politically and militarily. Since Roman dominance was achieved so much earlier in the south coastal region (121 B.C. in Provincia Narbonensis) than in the rest of Gaul (58-51 B.C.), one would expect extensive acculturation to have taken place at least a half-century before it was apparent in the rest of Gaul. However, even sites like Glanum, which was both a Greek and a Roman settlement, show the remarkable tenacity of indigenous modes of life.

The Roman drive to include Provincia Narbonensis in the Republic left Celtic strongholds on the southern coast either decimated (as was Entremont), incorporated into the Roman trade network and settled by Greek, and eventually (49 B.C.) Roman, colonials (as was Glanum), or overlooked in favor of more advantageously located cities (as was Ensérune).

Little demographic evidence is available from the archaeology because of the biased nature of the archaeological sampling, except that sites like Entremont continued to expand throughout their history, due partially to increasing urbanization along the coast and partially to a constant influx of traders and colonials. Economically, the south coastal area prospered throughout the Gaulish fight for independence; it had had tenuous ties with the Celtic world to the north (especially in the La Tène period) due to early Greek presence, and after 121 B.C. was bound to Roman economic fortunes. The non-Iberian, non-classical elements we are able to isolate are almost all attributable to Neolithic and Bronze Age survivals in the First Iron Age. During the Second Iron Age (La Tène III) Hallstatt survivals and vulgates of the Celtic styles popular in the north appear in south coastal sites.

Social Structure

The presence of colonials in the south coastal area is of utmost importance in any consideration of the region's social structure during La Tène III. Indigenous patterns were modified to correspond to those of the group in political control. This is particularly true in the case of the Romans who encouraged intermarriage, assumed many similarities between Celtic social structure and Rome's, and used extant Celtic institutions to carry out Roman policy. This amalgamation was apparently quite smooth for the Celtic aristocracy, which enthusiastically adopted Roman ways and names; but there is some evidence that among the lower classes the old gods and the old ways prevailed for some time.

RHÔNE CORRIDOR SITES

Celtic sites of La Tène in the Rhône corridor area of France are of primary importance to our study for three reasons. Most important, the Rhône-Saône river valley was the most effortless inland route to Britain and the north of Gaul. Secondly, a number of sites have been carefully excavated and they supply abundant data on certain aspects of Celtic social organization. Finally, although these habitations were in an important area of trade with the classical world, the emphasis was overwhelmingly indigenous, and thus we are provided with an excellent laboratory for observing acculturation.

Mont Lassois

Mont Lassois (or Montagne St-Marcel) (36) was an oppidum of the Lingones, on the heights north-northwest of Châtillon-sur-Seine and 100 meters from the River Seine. The plateau measures approximately 400 x 100 meters, has steep slopes, and is easily defensible. The site has produced evidence of an intensive Hallstatt occupation, followed by an occupational hiatus, then a La Tène III occupation; there was limited use of the plateau during Gallo-Roman times. Joffroy unearthed what he thinks is a true murus gallicus in 1952-53, but little other information on the La Tène III period of occupation is available. The Hallstatt occupation yielded the now-famous chariot burial of a Celtic princess, noted particularly for its treasures imported from the classical world; this gives us at least a sixth century date for a thriving trade route up the Rhône valley from the Mediterranean littoral.

Mont Auxois

Mont Auxois, or Alesia (37), was an important oppidum of the Mandubii. It is situated on a high, isolated promontory 150 meters above the valleys of the rivers Brenne, Ozerain, and Oze; it measures 97 hectares (239.6 acres) in area. The site was mentioned frequently by ancient authors and is best known from Caesar's account (*BG*, 7. 70 ff.) of his siege of Alesia in 52 B.C. and the defeat there of the Gaulish Confederacy and surrender of Vercingetorix. The main town was large, occupying most of the elongated ellipse of the plateau, 100 x 800 meters. Organized excavations were first undertaken in 1906; work between 1910-1912 demonstrated that the site had been extensively occupied in the Gaulish period and had continued to be occupied in a Gaulish manner under

Roman domination. The oldest Gallo-Roman houses have earlier Gaulish foundations. Isolated hearths of potters and metallurgists date from the Gaulish period. The numerous Gaulish huts found are assigned a date of first century B.C. A true murus gallicus serves as the enceinte's defensive wall. There is abundant evidence of Roman influence: there are theaters, baths, a civil basilica, a forum. The courtyard in front of the civil basilica yielded statuary of a tradition other than Greco-Roman; Le Gall (1963) suggests that this is evidence that indigenous sculptors did work similar to that recovered in Languedoc and in Provence (particularly from Entremont), and that perhaps these artists and workmen fled north from the Narbonne area (the consul M. Fulvius Flaccus destroyed Entremont in 124 B.C.) to areas in which their work found appreciation. At the same level was found an inscription in Greek characters but in the Gaulish language. This debris was above a Nero-Claudian pavement; it suggests that vestiges of Gaulish art and religion continued to exist well into the second century A.D. Further, two sanctuaries and a statue dedicated to the Gaulish goddess Damona, although dating to the second century A.D., are of types appropriate to indigenous Gaul, not Roman Gaul. The street plans of Alesia are confused and tend to follow the hill. There is no occupation earlier than La Tène III. The founding of Alesia seems to coincide with the Roman invasion of the Narbonne area and the invasions of the Cimbri and Teutones. The habitations are Gaulish by technique, but Gallo-Roman by date. One area seems to have been a quarter of the poor; near the contemporaneous cemetery, huts (measuring between 1.5 m x 4 m and 25 m x 4 m) were cut into the rock. Descent was by stairs carved into the rock. This area, called En Curiot, was inhabited just before or up to the second century A.D. Roman masonry was then perfectly known at Alesia. Its absence in this quarter and its presence in other richer areas near the city's center suggests a notable economic distinction among the inhabitants of Alesia.

The city's economic life is also amply reflected in its archaeology. Gallo-Roman farmers were numerous—many picks and spades, sickles, wheeled plows (a Gallic invention, according to Pliny the Elder), and small billhooks were recovered. Evidence for extensive wine-growing provides the beginning of the history of Burgundy. A great number of amphoras were recovered. Most, dating from the second century A.D., were Spanish and carried oil, olives, and fish sauce. Italian amphoras had all but disappeared by this time; Thévenot (1949) believes this is evidence that Burgundy wine had begun to be exported to Italy, or at least that Italian wine was no longer important to Gaul. There was an abundance of local wares and statuettes of fired clay.

There was also a brisk manufacture of iron shackles and a quarter for slaves, suggesting that Alesia may have served as a center of slave traffic by reason of its proximity to the German frontier. Nearby were metallurgical centers at Montbard and Ste. Colombe (near Châtillon-sur-Seine), which were still functioning until the third century A.D., and the metalworkers' quarter at Alesia was large. There were also craftsmen in leather, wood, and bone, renowned for their workmanship. Bronze-workers' shops and forges were found; analysis showed that the bronze had been made from copper and tin from Cornwall.

Ucuetis and Bergusia, divinities of metallurgists, were the subjects of the dedication on a vase and an inscription offered at Alesia by Martialis; so many types of tools were found in the metallurgists' quarter that they obviously represent the tool kits of many craftsmen and artisans. But perhaps most intriguing of all was the discovery of the crypt of a sanctuary of Ucuetis and Bergusia. The implications of this shrine as a corporative edifice, or guild hall, are of the greatest importance.

Bibracte

Bibracte (or Mont Beuvray) (38) is perhaps the most important indigenous Celtic site of the La Tène III period. Bibracte is mentioned in Caesar's *Commentaries (BG.* 1. 23) as a very large, well supplied oppidum of the Aedui. It is, in fact, the largest of continuously occupied La Tène III sites, measuring 135 hectares (333.6 acres). Mt. Beuvray is a granite mountain whose flanks are cut by three valleys of streams which are tributaries of the Loire basin. It is well situated to serve as the economic center of Gaul, as it is within easy reach of both the Loire and the Seine (the latter through the Yonne). The Aedui were old allies of the Romans and opposed them for the first time by joining the Gaulish Confederacy in 52 B.C., near the end of the war for Gaulish independence. When the Aedui joined the Gauls, it was at Bibracte that Vercingetorix called the assembly of all Gaul. A defeat followed and three Aeduan chiefs were taken prisoner, forcing Vercingetorix to take refuge at Alesia. Following the fall of Alesia, Caesar showed a certain compassion toward Bibracte and went there himself to receive its submission, establishing his own winter quarters there in 52-51 B.C.

Excavations at Bibracte began in 1865 with a grant from Napoleon III, under the primary direction of J. Gabriel Bulliot (until 1895) and Joseph Déchelette (1897-1901). The fortifications were impressive; Bulliot estimated that the walls had stood five meters high and were five kilometers in circumference. Wooden towers protected the main entrance, and a ditch outside the wall 11 meters wide and six meters deep apparently surrounded the entire enceinte.

Déchelette was the first to study the finds as a whole; he attributed the occupation to La Tène III and considered it a type-site for the period. He distinguished between indigenous and imported wares: the latter were mostly amphoras from Italy or the Narbonnais, some with potter's stamps, and yellow- or white-handled Italianate jugs. The chief indigenous wares were flat-based spherical pots with flat rims and a zone of incised decoration around the top of the body, three-legged cooking pots, and plain grey pots and plates. There were only a few sherds of the distinctive Roman Arretine, from the period of Caesar and Augustus.

The analysis of coins correlates with other data: the most active period of the occupation of the site was the second half of the first century B.C.; it was abandoned ca. 5 B.C. There were almost no Roman coins (42); some Celtiberian pieces and coins from other tribes were recovered. They appear to reflect greater frequency of trade to the north and east than to the south (Fig. 11).

The city of Bibracte was not laid out on a grid system, as is characteristic of classical cities, but it did have quarters or barrios, distinctive in function and types of inhabitants (Fig. 12). One quarter was devoted to the wealthy (Le Parc aux Chevaux), another to a civic and business district (Le Champlain), a third to a marketplace (La Chaume du Beuvray), a fourth served as a religious area (Le Teureau de la Wivre); a fifth section was a large industrial area (Le Come Chaudron), and a sixth an area of temporary housing (Pierre-Salvée, Theurot de la Roche). Two main roads, one for ascent from the northeast and the other to the southwest for descent, served the mountain top city. On the road used for ascent, the first area encountered was the industrial quarter. The excavations of 1868 exposed a blacksmith's shop made of earth and wood, with a thatched roof. It was without the sub-basement in stone which characterizes the more recent constructions in the oppidum. The street front measures 5.5 meters by 6.5 meters; set in the clay floor were great dressed slabs forming a resistant area 60 meters to a side, appropriate to the exigencies of the trade. Traditionally the anvil-block characteristic of Gaulish ironworks was fixed in a pit, where cremated remains of the blacksmith replaced forever the instrument of his labors. One descended into this two-meter-deep excavation by means of a ladder. The house of the smith, which apparently burned with little warning, contained 11 Gaulish medals and various tools. More important were the remains of an anvil, stone polishers, four whetstones, a chisel to cut off cold iron, a large lance twisted and out of its socket, sword fragments, numerous pieces of iron slag, a master key, nails of all dimensions, crucible fragments, pincers to seize the red-hot iron, and crucibles. One would hesitate to believe that people lived in these cramped quarters strewn with the tools of the shop had the excavations in 1867 not confirmed this.

The shop of a bronze founder with walls 2.8 meters to a side also yielded domestic materials. The east and west slopes of Le Come Chaudron were occupied by metallurgists of all sorts. The shop of a Gaulish enameller was excavated and yielded red enamel buttons, fibulae, and small cubes of opaque glass tinted red, blue, violet, black, and green. Gold, silver, and copper (as well as brass) were enamelled. Most enamellers' shops were in the Le Champlain area, lining either side of the street and of different sizes, situated between houses. The latter were square, most of them of wood, and some had gardens. There is good association between many of these houses and the workers in enamelling, bronze, silver, and gold.

THE ARCHAEOLOGICAL EVIDENCE

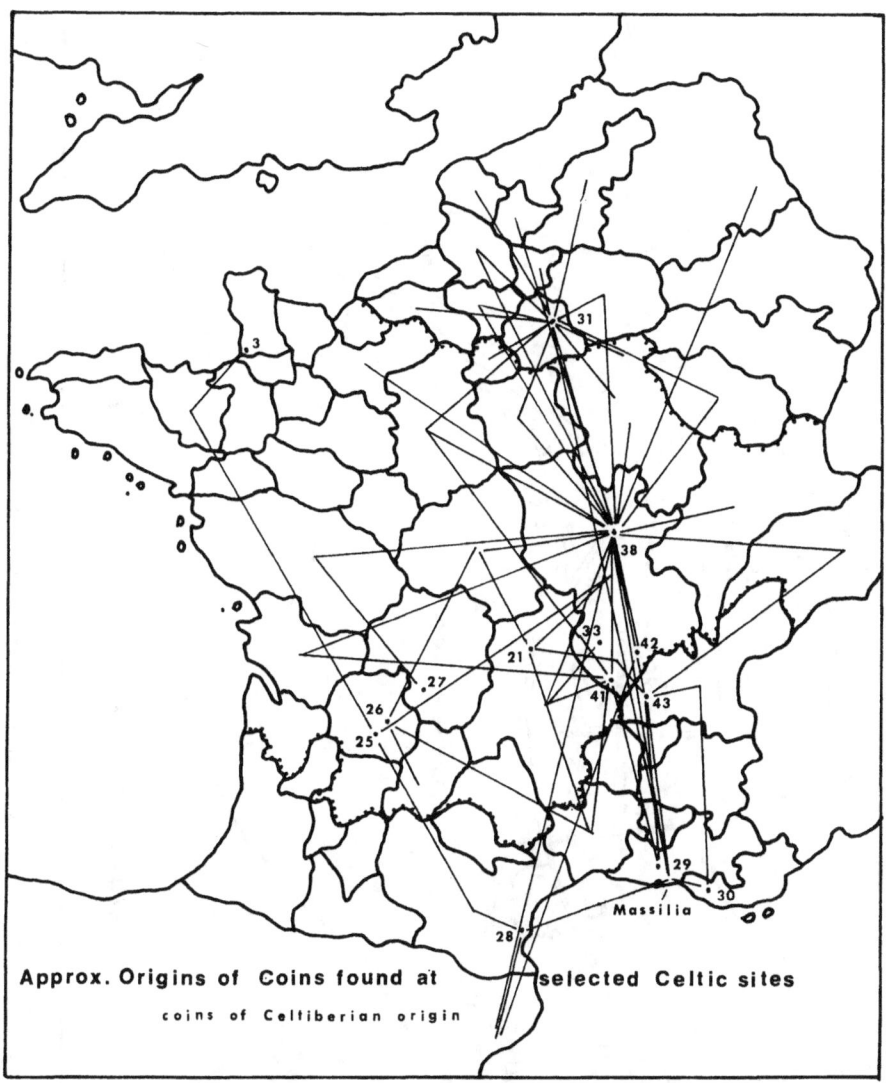

Fig. 11. Approximate Origins of Coins Found at Selected Sites.

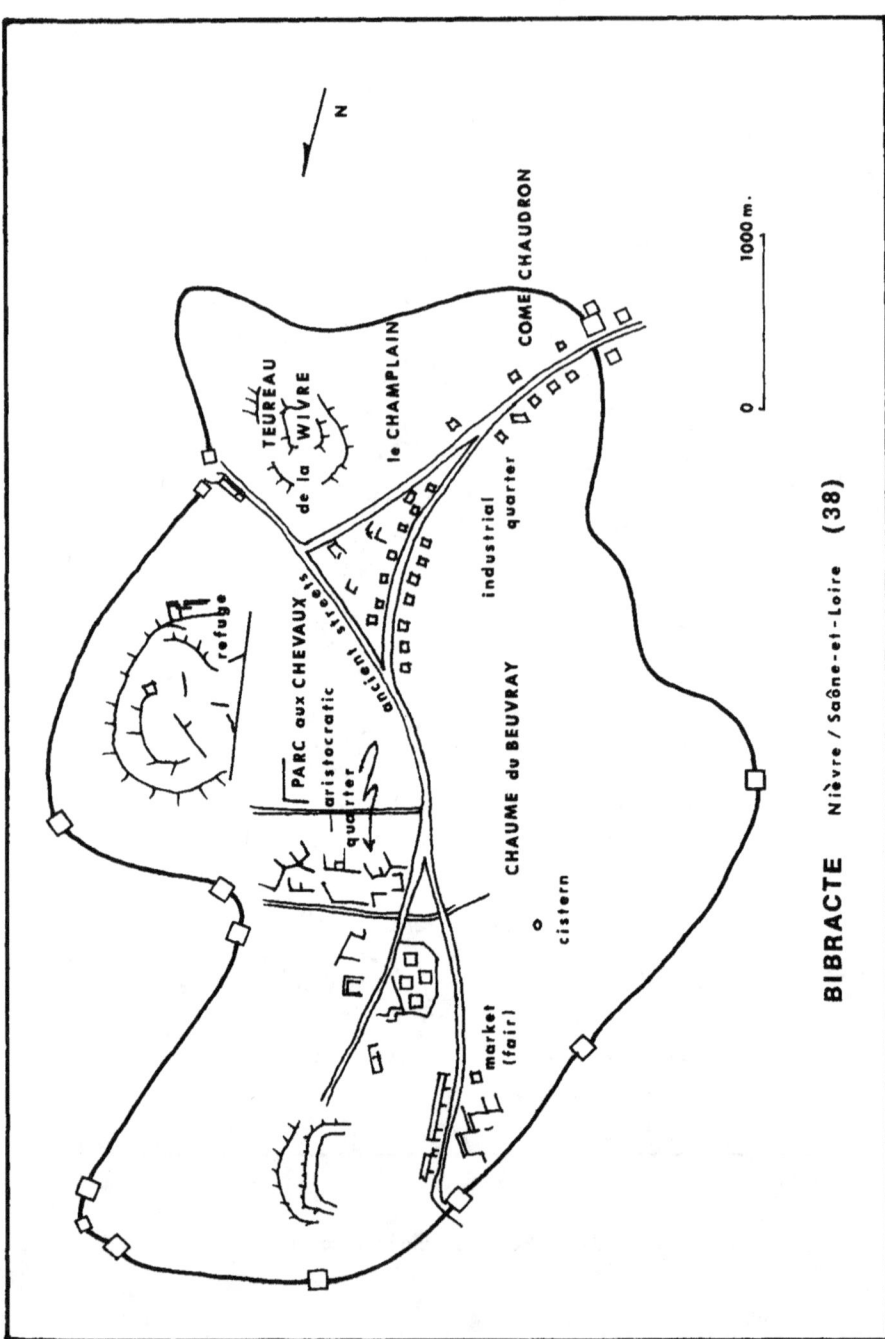

Fig. 12. Map of Excavations at Bibracte (38).

The ironworkers' shops and dwellings were primarily on the slopes of the Come Chaudron, although the distinction between the ironworkers and the others was apparently never clear-cut. A partial reason for the separation may have been the ironworkers' need for water in the forging process; five-meter-deep wooden conduits to the Come Chaudron from the southern end of the site provided a constant source of water for that purpose. The art of ironworking was well-known to the Gauls; they even manufactured steel girders somewhat resembling I-beams. All ornamentation motifs and weapon styles, etc., are Gaulish. Every aspect of this vast metalworking industry points to its Gaulish origin.

The area known as Le Teureau de la Wivre is thought to have been the place where Vercingetorix called the assembly of all Gaul in an attempt to unify the Gauls against Rome. Excavated evidence shows it to have been the *locus consecratus,* "consecrated place," where the senate (consilium) met. South and east of this area were found animal pens and corrals. The Parc aux Chevaux was obviously the quarter of wealthy Gauls. The largest house found there was 70 meters square, with an atrium, corridors, a large entrance, a number of apartments. It represents a way of life distinct from the preceding, but which is *not* Roman. The house is Gaulish, as much as those of Champlain and Come Chaudron. The architecture is more advanced, in a Mediterranean fashion, than in Gaul, but the constructions are Gaulish. The painting is sober, the mosaics simple, and lime is employed parsimoniously. There is no marble, there are no stone columns or capitals. Possibly, Bulliot suggests, the house was that of a Gaulish public figure. A second house, similar to the one described above but somewhat smaller, also belongs to the Gaulish epoch. It yielded no Imperial pottery and a single Roman coin. All other ceramics and coins recovered were of indigenous origin. It was furnished with a hypocaust, an under-floor heating system characteristic of Roman dwellings.

The Pierre-Salvée and Le Theurot de la Roche were separated from the Parc aux Chevaux by a solid stone wall. The area has little solid construction: there were only miserable huts, and evidence of shared quarters for man and beast. It served as a camp more than a permanent area of the city, a refuge for the landless and the pursued. La Chaume du Beuvray was the market quarter. There potters and other domestic merchants sold their goods, and fresh produce from the surrounding countryside was displayed in wooden stalls. This fair or market remained in operation even after the population was moved to Augustodunum (Autun) ca. 5 B.C. Most amazing of all, the fair has continued operation into the twentieth century. A photograph in Déchelette, *L'Oppidum de Bibracte* (1903), shows the fair amply attended in the late nineteenth century on the exact spot where it stood in the first century B.C. Many such aspects of Bibracte have interesting implications for the origins of distinguishing aspects of mediaeval society. Yet more important for this study, Bibracte is an illustration of a

Gaulish economic center at the peak of its importance, halfway through the first century B.C. Despite Mediterranean influence its aspect is overridingly indigenous.

Essalois

Essalois (41) was, at the end of Gaulish independence, a great exchange center which imported into the Loire valley goods from Italy and the Rhône valley. As a result of its location not far from the frontier of the Provincia Romana, it controlled this zone of transit. Amphoras were found similar (even to the potters' marks) to those at Bibracte and the quantity was proportionately greater. Indigenous ceramics were also very similar. Wheeler and Richardson (1957) believe the comparable elements in design motifs between ceramics at the two sites denote a school using the same styles and methods of manufacture in the different tribes (Aedui and Segusiavi), or perhaps nomadic workers moving from one to another. Bulliot (1899) thought Essalois, like Bibracte, to have been a market town with an industrial quarter. Coins from Marseille were found while (as at Bibracte) Roman Imperial coinage was absent. Gaulish coins were primarily those of the Aedui and the Segusiavi, but coins of the Arverni, Carnutes, and Santones were present and give evidence of a commercial liaison between these tribes. Preynat (1962) believes, on the basis of coins and ceramics, that Essalois (41) dates from 180 B.C. to 30 B.C.

Le Crêt Châtelard

The most distinctive features of Le Crêt Châtelard (42) are rubbish or water-storage pits scattered through the enclosed area. Most were cylindrical, with an average depth of five meters. Pit fillings were a fine gray clayish silt which in turn contained well-preserved wood, nuts, and fruits (prunes, raisins, and figs). Also recovered were a cylindrical wooden box and a carved statuette. Ceramics of pre-Roman and Roman date were found, the former resembling types from Bibracte. But the most important ceramic finds were vessels painted in geometric designs. Durand (1899) noted that although this pottery is found elsewhere in Gaul, nowhere is it more abundant than in the oppida of the Segusiavi. The pits themselves are associated with the Gaulish occupation. Le Crêt Châtelard was a Gaulish oppidum late in the period of independence and a flourishing city in the Roman period, but was deserted before the onset of the barbarian invasions.

Pommiers

The site of Pommiers (31) was an important oppidum of the Suessiones. Its inhabitants produced iron tools, weapons, and ornaments in quantity, and minted their own coinage. Over 700 coins have been recovered from all over Gaul (see Fig. 11). The coin data suggest that Pommiers served groups in the surrounding area as a regional trade center, passing to southern points such raw material as tin and iron, and receiving finished and luxury items in return.

Vienne

The Allobrogian site of Vienne (43) is situated on the hill of Ste. Blandine between the plains of Lyon and Valence, in the Rhône valley; it is near the confluence of the Rhône and Gere rivers. It was a major commercial site in La Tène III times, and may have been the city Strabo mentions (*Geographia,* IV, I, 11). It has been excavated periodically since 1895, most recently in 1955-1965, and the finds reported by Chapotat (1970). A careful artifact analysis tells us much about activities in Gallic and Gallo-Roman Vienne. It was obviously an active trade link between central Gaul and the Mediterranean world, as reflected by Campanian, Greek, and Roman ceramics and Roman coins. It was a market center in one of the richest agricultural regions of Gaul, as evidenced by a rich array of farming tools: scythes, sickles, billhooks, forks, hoes, and shovels as well as prods and chains for handling domestic animals. Vienne was also an active industrial center, with bronzeworking, ironworking and smelting, leatherworking and boneworking, as represented by tools and finished materials of those trades. The materials recovered at Vienne correlate with La Tène III artifacts from Alesia (37), Bibracte (38), Ensérune (28), Entremont (30), Gergovia (21), Murcens (26), Puy du Tour (27), and Puy d'Issolu (24).

Settlement System, Demography, and Economy

The Rhône corridor area of France was perhaps the most important economic area in Gaul; the Rhône-Saône river system was navigable as far north as Bibracte, where a short journey connected travellers with the Loire and Seine systems, as well as the less important rivers of the interior. More than the northern or western areas, the culture history of this corridor region was influenced by its location on the most heavily-travelled trade route in western Europe. The sixth century B.C. Hallstatt finds at Vix underscore the early importance of the route for commerce with the classical world, and this link with the Mediterranean grew even more heavily travelled during the La Tène period.

Inevitably, the result of such extensive free trade was political stratification on the basis of wealth, which in turn brought to prominence throughout Gaul the tribes inhabiting the region. The Aedui, whose main fortress was Bibracte, and the Sequani were early allies (121 B.C.) of Rome, who feared that the tribes' position astride the trade route might someday threaten Roman commerce. Only when Caesar was defeated at Gergovia by the Arvernian

Vercingetorix did the careful and political Aedui desert Caesar's legions and join the national rebellion against Rome.

Despite extensive trade relationships with the classical world before and after the conquest, the sites in the Rhône corridor area have a strongly indigenous character. Apparently the groups in the area had adjusted well to a symbiotic relationship with Mediterranean powers without abandoning their own autonomy. Ample evidence exists that art, architecture, industry, language, and religion were essentially Gaulish not only before the conquest, but for at least a half century thereafter. Most of the sites reviewed here continued to be occupied for some time after the conquest, at least until Augustus ordered the hillforts abandoned near the close of the first century B.C.

There were a number of important trade centers in the Rhône corridor area, many of which also served as tribal capitals. The population density was high both before and after the conquest, if we may use size comparisons of pre- and post-conquest occupations, and the low frequency of site abandonment. Most of these centers would assuredly qualify as *poleis,* or cities; Pounds (1971: 24) defines *polis* as "a walled enclosure, on rising ground, dominated by a fortress or acropolis and . . . commanding a view out over its own fields. . . . Within the walls would be narrow streets lined with houses, small and simply built . . . a public square or *agora,* and a few public buildings, which alone would show any architectural distinction." One might add to that definition the archaeological evidence of sharp functional distinctions among areas of the site.

Social Structure

These Rhône corridor sites provide the best information available on Celtic social structure. Huge sites like Bibracte and Alesia were the flower of Celtic urban life and give us invaluable information on the increasingly sophisticated class and status differentiations within a society moving rapidly toward statehood. The contemporaneous existence of quarters for the rich, the well-to-do (who may have been merchants and petty officials), the poor and the destitute (as at Bibracte) speaks for the existence of at least three and perhaps four classes: the governing aristocracy, a middle class of merchants, civil employees, and guild members of the skilled trades, followed by agriculturalists, and finally a group of refugees and the destitute who may have worked as jobbers in agriculture and industry. Status distinctions are reflected by the relative wealth of the homes of some members of the trades as compared to others practicing the same occupation. Obviously in this area in La Tène III the simplistic class distinctions made by Caesar are inapplicable; it is demonstrable archaeologically that before the Roman conquest Gaul, and especially the Rhône corridor area, had attained many of the characteristics of statehood, and the social complexities that statehood implies.

Celtic Social Structure—Archaeological Evidence

Archaeological evidence for Celtic social structure suggests a notable differentiation in complexity for the five regions studied. The north coastal area undoubtedly had the least complex social structure in Gaul during the period before the conquest; the inhabitants were scattered, the population density was low, and there were no centers of regional trade for which we have evidence. The nature of the social structure is problematical, but the presence of locally minted coinage and large, elaborate fortifications (apparently intended as group refuges) suggests at least a tribal (Service, 1972) level of organization. The west-central area had not only fortified camps and refuges, but regional trading centers as well, which suggest an active system of trade and high population density. Evidence derived from excavation in the regional centers reveals a complex social stratification including an aristocracy, artisans, agriculturalists, civil employees, merchants, and a host of petty officials. Through the southwestern area lay the Aquitanian Way, a major trade route in western Europe. It is not surprising that we also find regional centers of trade, and evidence there of an aristocracy, artisans, and agriculturalists. The south coastal area, due to the early, documented presence of colonials, represents a region already extensively acculturated. The area had been a center of trade since the sixth century B.C., when Marseille became a Greek port of trade. Archaeological data (especially architectural) reflect widespread adoption of classical elements among the aristocracy, but the presence of certain indigenous features suggests that Romanization had a differential impact: the lower classes held to old gods and old ways considerably longer than the upwardly mobile aristocracy, thrust into a direct competition for status with colonials. The Rhône corridor area gives the best evidence for the existence of a complex indigenous Gaulish social structure before the conquest. The archaeological evidence clearly indicates the presence of an aristocracy, a middle class of merchants and skilled specialists who were guildsmen, and a lower class composed of rural agriculturalists who used the centers as produce depots and the urban destitute who inhabited the centers' ghettos. That these centers were cities seems certain; the distinctive groups represented in the population of all cities, even including the ubiquitous urban poor, are represented in the archaeology of the centers of pre-conquest Gaul.

The archaeological evidence pertaining to Celtic social structure reflects (1) the limiting effects of the environment on the peoples of the desolate north coast where restricted resources and distance from the main routes of trade and concomitant low population density mitigated against the emergence of a complex social structure; (2) the differential impact of culture contact on the aristocracy of the south coastal region as contrasted with its lower classes; and (3) the effect long-distance trade had in increasing social stratification along the trade routes and in areas of valuable natural resources (the west-central, southwestern, and Rhône corridor regions), due to a wider distribution of wealth.

Although Gaul at the time of the conquest did not exhibit everywhere an homogeneous class structure, a pattern of stratification may be observed in at least three regions: west-central, southwestern, and the Rhône corridor. There is evidence for at least three internally stratified classes: an aristocracy, an emergent middle class of artisans, bureaucrats and merchants, and a lower class of rurally-based agriculturalists and urban migrants.

Some of the data from urban centers in Gaul suggest even further class distinctions, especially in the middle and lower classes. It is certain, for example, that at Bibracte the social distance was great between artisans in various quarters of the city, but the applicability of such findings to other areas is, on the whole, unknown. Similarly, it is interesting to speculate about the role of mercantilism in the breakdown of the rigid two-class structure: did petty aristocrats or ambitious peasants predominate in the merchant class? Did one control long-range trade and the other local transactions? Another distinction might also be made (on the basis of the temporary housing found at Bibracte) between rural agriculturalists and what appear to be migrant laborers. It is tempting to postulate a full-blown pluralistic society for at least some sophisticated urban areas of Gaul, but conclusive proof must await further excavation.

PART III

GENERAL CONCLUSIONS

V

CRITICAL ANALYSIS OF LITERARY AND ARCHAEOLOGICAL DATA

CLASSICAL literary sources mention only two classes in Celtic society: (1) an internally stratified aristocracy, consisting of two sub-groups with distinctive functions, one administrative and moral (Druides) and the other military (equites); and (2) commoners, or plebs. It is obvious from the archaeological data that Celtic society was extensively stratified, and that probably one other class existed, counting as members minor administrative officials, skilled tradesmen, and merchants. It is also apparent that, like the aristocracy in which are found numerous role and status possibilities, the middle and lower classes also had internal distinctions.

Caesar not only failed to mention the existence of intermediate categories of stratification, but also said little about the functions which individuals in these intermediate positions must have fulfilled in Celtic society. This may have been for several reasons. Tierney (1960:212) has established that the bulk of Caesar's information on Celtic ethnography comes from earlier sources, namely Posidonius (ca. 135-51/50 B.C.). In all likelihood, Posidonius wrote his Celtic ethnography (book 23, the *Histories*) about 60 years before Caesar utilized his observations. During the intervening period (approximately two generations), this study suggests that Celtic society was undergoing a marked change in social structure as a response to a wider distribution of wealth. This "trickle effect" (see Introduction, and Fallers, 1966:403) would appear to have been the result of increased trade into Celtic Gaul after the loss of transalpine Gaul to the Romans and the establishment of Provincia Narbonensis in 121 B.C. Posidonius' bias in favor of the *nobilitas* and his vindication in the *Histories* of Roman imperialism (OCD, 1970) was obviously shared by Caesar, and although it is unlikely that Caesar had any clear conception of the ideas of Posidonius, he was impressed by his work (Tierney, 1960:213) and drew heavily upon it. Further, Caesar had little interest in Gallic ethnography as such, and included it because he knew it to be an accepted part of historiography and an important smokescreen for his defeats in 53 B.C. It was also to Caesar's advantage to portray Celtic society as consisting of a relatively disorganized and internally divided, but powerful elite governing a discontented lower class.

It is not likely that Caesar was unaware of the emergent Celtic middle class and saw only the commoners in the fields and the aristocracy in conflict or negotiation. He camped at Bibracte during the winter of 52-51 B.C. and must have seen the extensive artisan's quarters and the houses of bureaucrats and merchants.

The presently available archaeological data give us no indication of the internal stratification of the aristocracy into equites and three categories of Druides; the archaeology shows only that there was an aristocracy whose functions were governmental and quite possibly religious and moral. Further, the archaeology does not indicate the existence of the patron-client relationship, which is the keystone for understanding the mechanisms of the Celtic transition from what may have been a petty chiefdom level of organization to statehood. It is also obvious that without the literary evidence, archaeologists might have concluded that invasion and conquest took place from the ubiquitous defenses throughout Gaul and the unfinished character of some of them, but the routes of conquest and the particular historical and political situations which led to this invasion would have been lost. Archaeologists might do well to look somewhat further afield for the reasons for invasion: in this case, a request (by Gaulish groups near the Rhine) for aid and protection from a third group (the Germans) put Gaul in direct conflict with her champion by giving Rome opportunity for invasion with an easy excuse for initial occupation and ready political allies within Gaul.

COMPOSITE MODEL: CELTIC SOCIAL STRUCTURE

At the time of the conquest, Celtic society was highly stratified, and an emerging multiple-class system of at least three distinct levels can be discerned. An aristocracy, a middle class, and a lower class were each internally stratified on the basis of both ascribed status (kinship, sex) and, increasingly important, achieved status (occupation, wealth, personal exploits).

At the beginning of the period under study, ascribed status was more important than achieved status and political and social organization were solidly kin-based. As increased trade made wealth available to members of all classes and the patron-client relationship replaced kinship as a basis for political integration, social mobility was increased, and achieved status (within the limits of class) became a more common basis for social stratification. The flexibility of class boundaries is difficult to determine, but the data suggest that the system of patronage as practiced between the upper and lower classes in the area of craftsmanship, plus expanding markets for the products of these specialists, led to an autonomous middle class, made up initially of artisans but soon joined by merchants and bureaucrats, and drawn from what was formerly the lower class. It is suggested here that this internal change in social structure, precipitated by the input of classical wealth into the Celtic economic system, is a critical mechanism in the rise of the secondary state.

HYPOTHESES GENERATED BY AN ANALYSIS OF CELTIC SOCIAL STRUCTURE

A number of closely related questions have emerged from this study, many of which will be answered through continued research in the area. Demographic and settlement system data may be obtained by site survey in regions selected (on the basis of availability of data) here, as well as those areas (such as the extreme southwest) where little information is presently available. By surveying the areas for all sites of La Tène II/III date, whatever their size or function, one would gain valuable information on population distribution and settlement systems, trade networks and sociopolitical organization.

I. Demography and Settlement System
  A. The density of settlement in the La Tène II/III period is a function of local environmental conditions and distance from major trade routes.
    1. Environmental Conditions
      a. *Climate*
      The more closely regional climatic conditions approximate Mediterranean climate conditions, the greater the population density.
      b. *Resources*
      The greater the store of natural resources in the region (Sn, Ag, Au, Cu, Fe), the greater the population density.
      c. *Terrain*
      The more accessible an area is to other areas (water routes, easy land crossings, ports), the greater the population density.
      d. *Integration of Conditions*
      The interaction of the above factors (a, b, c) determines the primacy of a region in terms of population density and economic activity.
    2. Distance from Major Trade Routes
      a. *River Systems*
      The major river systems of France correlate directly with the areas of population density.

1. The Rhône-Saône river system, connecting with most of the other major rivers in France, will be of greatest importance.
2. The Garonne River/Aquitanian Gap system and the Loire/Cher/Allier river system will be of somewhat lesser importance.
   b. *Ports of Trade*
   Marseille and other ports of trade on the Mediterranean seacoast in *Provincia Narbonensis* will be of focal importance as the initial link of Gaul with the Mediterranean trade network.
3. Density of Settlement by Area
   a. The north coastal region will be of lowest population density.
   b. The extreme southwest will be of next lowest population density.
   c. The west central and northern southwestern regions will be of moderate population density.
   d. The Rhône corridor region will be of high population density.
   e. The south coastal region will be of highest population density.
B. The density of settlement correlates with the level of complexity of the social structure.
   1. The north coastal region will be least complex.
   2. The southwestern region will be of somewhat greater complexity.
   3. The west central region will be of moderate complexity.
   4. The Rhône corridor region will be most complex of the autonomous Gaulish regions.
   5. The south coastal region will be very complex, but in a specialized colonial sense.
C. Site type is determined by its function; site function is determined by geographical, economic and political factors.
   1. Site Types
      a. *Refuge*
         function: will serve scattered transhumant populations under threat of attack.

ex.:
Camp d' Artus (1)

         location: will be common in the north coastal, west central and southwestern areas, on Caesar's anticipated line of march, or low population density.

LITERARY AND ARCHAEOLOGICAL DATA   79

  b. *Hamlet or Village*
   function: will serve as collection and production point for locally exchanged products and as the residence of agriculturalists.

ex.:
no published
examples

   location: will be common throughout agricultural areas of Gaul.
  c. *Fortified Town*
   function: will serve as collection and production center for inter- and intra-regional trade and as the residence of members of the aristocracy, craftsmen and specialists, government officials, some agriculturalists.

ex.:
Pommiers (31)

   location: will be central to a large area which includes a variety of natural resources and will have access to major trade routes.
  d. *Fortified City*
   function: will serve as a collection, production, and relay center for inter- and intra-regional trade and a collection, production and relay center for international trade.

ex.:
Bibracte (38)

   location: on a major trade route.
  e. *Port of Trade* (after Polanyi, et al., 1957)
   function: will serve as a national collection and relay center, but primarily as a communication center for two or more trading blocs through neutrally administered trade; presence of colonials.

ex.:
Marseille
(see site map),
Glanum (29)

   location: at the geographical point of articulation of two or more trading blocs.
 2. Evidence of interaction between sites will be archaeological and literary.
  a. *Numismatic Data* (see Fig. 23)
   1. Coins minted in one area of Gaul and found in another are evidence of a trade relationship.
   2. The number of coins found belonging to one group in the excavation of a site belonging to another is directly related to the intensity of trade between the two.
   3. In the coin evidence, fortified towns will be distinguished from fortified cities by more numerous coins from areas nearby (towns) or at considerably greater distance (cities).
   4. Ports of trade will yield coin inventories from throughout Gaul and the classical world.
  b. *Artifacts* resulting from interaction with Mediterranean trading blocs (ex.: ceramics).

c. *Commentary* by contemporary observers, e.g., Caesar on the functions of Bibracte (38).

II. Trade and Socio-Political Organization

A. Greek penetration into the interior of Gaul was limited to an articulation with Gaulish interregional trade due to the neutral nature of Marseille as a port of trade.

B. Roman penetration into the interior of Gaul was more ambitious than that of Greece, particularly after the south coastal area became *Provincia Narbonensis* in 121 B.C., due to the presence of the Roman army and numerous colonials.

C. As Roman interaction in Celtic regional trade and demand for Celtic goods increased, the Celts underwent a period of "primitive industrialization" to meet the demand.

D. The increased demand for goods destined for foreign export vastly increased the importance of artisans and craftsmen in Celtic society.

E. There was a concomitant increase in the demand among high-status individuals within Gaul for goods from the classical world.

F. This increased demand, linked with the "trickle effect" (low status people in league with industry devalue goods symbolic of high status by obtaining them and force high status individuals to seek other high-status-symbolic goods [Fallers, 1966:403]) increases the competition for status goods throughout the Celtic social structure.

G. The increased competition for status goods at all levels of Celtic social structure leads to a wider distribution of wealth and greater social stratification.

H. The patron-client relationship takes on a new facet of importance, and becomes "party directed" patronage. *Note:* Weingrod (1968: 381) defines two types of patronage. *Patron-client* ties can be seen to arise within a state structure in which considerable separation exists between the levels of village, city and state. *Party-directed* patronage is associated with the expanding scope and general proliferation of state activities, and also with the growing integration of village, city and state (in this case, as a result of organized trade networks linking regions).

I. Thus, Gaulish political organization becomes party-based rather than kin-based within the period La Tène II/III.

J. Gaul at the time of the conquest may be considered a primitive state, as defined by Service (1972:498-99).

APPENDIX I

ANCIENT ETHNOGRAPHIC SOURCES ON THE CELTS AND THEIR RELATIONSHIPS

Scientific interest in the world about them appeared early in Greek literary tradition: the poetry of Homer (ca. 750 B.C.) and the prose of Hecataeus (fifth century B.C.) reflect the long-standing popularity of geographical/ethnographical literature known as *periodoi* or *periegeseis* or *periploi*. The earliest surviving texts suitable for ethnographic analysis are those of Herodotus (ca. 484-424 B.C.). Born in Halicarnassus, a Dorian colony in Asia Minor, he travelled extensively throughout the whole world of his time and recorded in his *Histories* details of geography, settlement, and subsistence systems, observations on the language, race, clothing, customs, and group character of the inhabitants of the lands he visited. He appears to have had a model of organization in mind that is reflected in the orderly presentation and sensible subdivisions of his data. Karl Trüdinger (cited in Tierney, 1960) has proposed the following as Herodotus' model.

I. The Country
   1. Boundaries, measurements, shape
   2. Nature of the land
   3. Rivers
   4. Climate
   5. Animals
II. The People
   1. Population
   2. Antiquity
   3. Way of life
   4. Customs
III. Wonders of the Country

The fifth century was characterized by the emergence of theories of cultural and economic evolution; Hippocrates (ca. 460-399 B.C.), fifth century physician and contemporary of Socrates, dealt more thoroughly with certain aspects of ethnography missing from Herodotus' treatment, namely physical appearance and temperament or character; he saw these variations as an ultimate function of climate. We find this approach in Hippocrates' *Airs, Waters and Places*. Fourth-century Athenians continued an interest in history and ethnography, as their attempts to explain cultural phenomena grew more sophisticated. Fourth-century philosophers and historians also brought a more pragmatic approach to the history of non-literate peoples. While Herodotus and others of his period constructed histories based on a combination of ethnographic theory and likely tales, the fourth century was characterized by the use of principles, evidence, and inference in cultural analysis (Cole, 1967:146-47). This more practical mode of thought was in part due to a desire to apply various theories of organization, especially in government and politics (e.g., Plato's *Republic*). The theme of degeneration and decay, both in the individual and in the state, was a familiar one in fourth century history and philosophy; it was also an indication of the popularity of the concept of primitivism among fourth century thinkers (Tierney, 1960:190-91).

Primitivism represents a body of thought and attitudes more civilized groups entertain about those less advanced; to wit, that the earliest period of human history was the best, or that the acquisitions of civilization are evil. The former has been designated "chronological" primitivism by Lovejoy and Boas (1935), and is best exemplified by Hesiod's description of the Golden Age (ca. 700 B.C.). Thought to be of great antiquity, the Golden Age was replaced by "Ages" of increasingly more decadent men, both morally and physically the inferiors of the inhabitants of the Golden Age. According to Lovejoy and Boas, Hesiod's chronological primitivism is rarely found in later antiquity apart from the second type, "cultural" primitivism. In this view, earlier ways of life are considered more "natural" than the increasingly technological society of the day. It is difficult for twentieth century man, struggling with the problems of industrialization and a rapidly deteriorating environment, to believe that any Greeks could have thought their society burdened with evils wrought by civilization; in actuality one of the strongest and most persistent factors in Western thought is the use of the term "nature" to express a standard of human values and the identification of good with that which is "natural." Cole (1967) identifies two major currents in Greek thought: primitivism, and the so-called Myth of Human Progress, which is essentially a more positivist view of civilization and the changes it wrought on "natural" man. Advocates of the idea of progressivism were not numerous until the fourth century B.C., although the two currents appear to have been juxtaposed from the earliest period of Greek literature. The late fifth and early fourth centuries saw the rise of rationalism and the scientific method, and until that time (due to primitivism's intrinsic support of certain Greek religious beliefs) the idea of human progress was not a popular one.

Lovejoy and Boas make a further distinction between types of cultural primitivism: "soft" primitivists saw an original life of simplicity and virtue as eclipsed by their own more complex but intrinsically less worthy one; "hard" primitivists were unresponsive to this romantic and idealized concept of the barbarian and did not minimize his uncivilized customs. The concept of primitivism is central to a discussion of classical ethnographic tradition, as it colors all accounts of peoples peripheral to the Graeco-Roman world.

While the Greek ethnographic tradition was a product of early philosophical interests as well as practicality, the Roman tradition responded more to the pragmatic needs of the Roman state. From earliest times, Rome had excelled in government; whole areas of Latin literature grew up in answer to some practical need, edifying, and in the service of a national ideal. Literature was of little importance compared to Roman political and economic concerns, and Latin prose literature was dominated by oratory and history. Ethnographic material from these sources, although completely different in character from the Greek, is equally valuable. Roman sources may have had a purpose other than pure description, but nonetheless they included much the same type of information provided by Herodotus. Cato (the Elder, 234 B.C.-149 B.C.) was the first major Roman historian to include ethnographic material. Some of Cato's successors (e.g., Cicero) followed Cato's example in including social and religious information, but most followed the strict annalistic form of the priestly chronicles.

The best synopsis of ancient Celtic ethnography is in Tierney (1960), and is followed here. The earliest ethnographic material on the Celts in Western Europe is a *Periplus,* or detailed account of coastal sailing (recorded by Avienus in the fourth century A.D.) which dates to the early fifth century B.C. It was written by or for a Massiliote merchant, and describes the coast between Cadiz and Marseille, but its main value as a document for those interested in the Celts is that it verifies the presence of Celtic tribes on the North Sea, in France, and southwestern Spain in the early fifth century B.C. This correlates with linguistic and archaeological evidence of Celtic presence in Spain by the seventh century and even earlier in France and on the Rhine.

Hecataeus is the first known author to mention the Celts, in a geographical work written ca. 500 B.C. Herodotus also mentions them as living on the upper Danube, near the Pyrenees and in farther Spain, in his *Histories* (ca. 428 B.C.). The fourth century B.C. yielded scanty ethnographic material on the Celts. Xenophon mentions that the Celts were used as mercenaries by the tyrant Dionysius of Syracuse; Plato names the Celts as one of six barbarian warlike peoples; Asclepiades of Tragilos mentions a Celtic king; Pseudo-Scylax speaks of a Celtic tribe at the head of the Adriatic.

Aristotle, writing in about 330 B.C., discusses Celtic customs at length, and the historian Ephorus classifies the Celts as the major peripheral nation to the west of the classical world. Theopompus, also an historian, relates the capture of

Rome by the Gauls, and his writings generally reflect the advance of the Celts toward the Balkans at the end of the fourth century B.C. Another anonymous geographer, Pseudo-Scymnus, mentions the wealth of the Celtic countries in tin, gold, and copper and the extensive adoption of Greek ways by the Spanish Celts. The navigator Pytheas, writing ca. 310-306 B.C., also adds considerable geographical information on the Celts. He was one of the sources of Timaeus, Eratosthenes, and Hipparchus. Ptolemy, Hieronymus of Cardia, the historian Phylarchus, and the poet Sopater, all writing ca. 270-260 B.C., mention Celtic customs. Polybius (ca. 200-post-118 B.C.), of the earlier (second and third centuries, B.C.) group of authors who dealt with Celtic material, is the most voluminous. His information touches not only on geography and mores but social structure and religion as well.

The Celtic ethnography of Posidonius, however, is the most extensive and represents the highest level of achievement in both Celtic ethnography and Greek ethnography as a whole. Posidonius (135-51 B.C.) wrote a *History,* which is not itself extant, but is (with some changes and additions) quoted extensively by three later Greek authors: the historian Diodorus Siculus, the geographer Strabo, and the writer of miscellanies, Athenaeus. Caesar apparently also used Posidonius as a source, without acknowledgment. Tierney (1960:198) says that very little ethnographic material in later writers on the Celts comes from sources other than these four authors mentioned, and ultimately, most comes from Posidonius. Thus, the so-called Posidonian tradition of "hard" primitivism, with special reference to Celts, "represents a policy pledged to uphold the Roman imperial attitude unsympathetic to a foreign barbaric society" (Chadwick, 1966: 27). Figure 13 indicates further relationships between initiators of the Posidonian tradition and later authors from whom we have information on the Celts.

In addition to information from first century B.C. authors deriving the bulk of their material from Posidonius, it has been suggested that there exists another tradition less well-documented and considerably more controversial. As far as we know, none of the material in this so-called Alexandrian tradition appears in the works of writers who had been in Gaul; instead it was preserved from an earlier period by scholars educated in the School at Alexandria from at least as early as the first century A.D. Although many classical scholars would disagree, Chadwick (1966:58) says that for the above reasons this tradition has either been overlooked or treated as late in origin and therefore unimportant. Chadwick insists that evidence from the sources themselves ascertains that much of this Alexandrian material is at least as early as the tradition derived from Posidonius, and that some of it is apparently earlier. It may even represent remnants of works of those whom Havelock (1957) would call the Greek liberals, philosophers with an anthropological orientation who predated Plato and Aristotle. But the major importance of the work of the Alexandrians, the question of the antiquity of their philosophical origins notwithstanding, lies in its

APPENDIX I 85

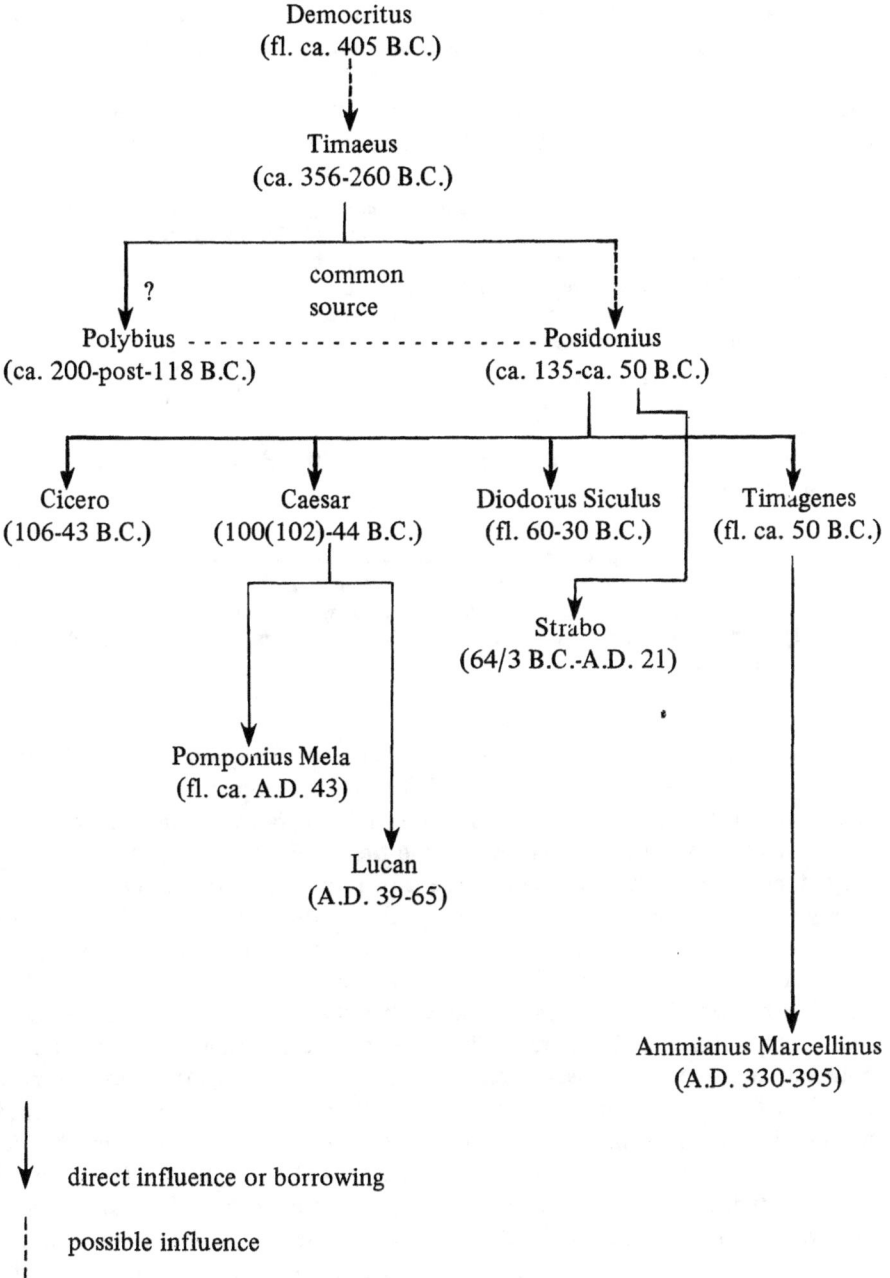

Fig. 13. The Posidonian Tradition.

attitudinal contrast to the Posidonian tradition. The Alexandrians are respectful of Druidic philosophy and cite parallels throughout the classical world; the Posidonians incorporate many elements unfavorable to the Druids as a class and the Celts as a people, such as their "barbaric" rites. For example, Diogenes Laertius, associated with the Alexandrians, comments thus on the Druids:

> There are some who say that the study of philosophy had its beginnings among the barbarians. They urge that the Persians have had their Magi, the Babylonians or Assyrians their Chaleaeans, and the Indians their Gymnosophists; and among the Celts and Gauls there are the people called Druids or Holy Ones, for which they cite as authorities the *Magicus* of Aristotle and Sotion in the twenty-third book of his Succession of Philosophers.
>
> (I, 1 [this parallels Clement of Alexandria *Stromata* i.71])

In contrast, Diodorus Siculus, representative of the Posidonian tradition, says this about the Druids:

> . . . when two armies approach each other in battle with swords drawn and spears thrust forward, these men step forth between them and cause them to cease, as though having cast a spell over certain kinds of wild beasts. In this way, even among the wildest barbarians, does passion give place before wisdom and Ares stands in awe of the Muses.
>
> (V.31.3-5)

There is little contradiction of fact between the two quotations or the two classes of evidence (Chadwick, 1966:59), but the emphasis and climate are totally different. Both Posidonian and Alexandrian traditions are representative of the attitude of cultural primitivism, the first hard, the second soft. Together, they stand in contrast to the more ardent of progressivist traditions. This is not to say that we consistently find a simplistic picture of hard vs. soft primitivist attitudes among writers who mention the Celts, or even that some writers express both, or neither, or use the Celts as contrasting examples to the "progress" of the classical world. Yet we must realize that the two sentiments exist side by side as an adjunct to the literary climate of any age. Certain sets of economic, political, and social circumstances recur; one or the other attitude may be more prevalent for a time. For example, the popular mid-nineteenth century attitude toward the American Indian was primarily one of hard primitivism; but by the end of the century the romanticism of the so-called Noble Savage (a variety of soft primitivism) was undoubtedly more popular. It is a lamentable but verifiable observation that the greater the dominance in an acculturation situation of one group over another, the more prevalent an attitude of "soft" primitivism on the part of the dominant group.

APPENDIX II

ADDITIONAL SITE DATA

Information on Celtic sites of La Tène III along the north coast of France has been taken from Wheeler and Richardson (1957) unless otherwise indicated. Their field crews made an extensive survey of the area and excavated five of the enceintes discovered which appeared most promising. Wheeler and Richardson's analysis of excavation and survey data yielded three major types of fortification. The first, tribal oppida of the "Petit Celland" series, is characterized by unfinished defenses, the burning of the main gate, abundant Gaulish coins, and a position on an arterial passage between the highlands and the sea. Le Camp d'Artus (1) and Le Châtellier (3) are of this type. Wheeler and Richardson see such sites as the response of scattered tribesmen in regions of low population density to the threat of Roman conquest (ca. 56 B.C.): they rallied at a central point, hastily fortified the site, and armed themselves on a formidable scale. It was a consistent response from the Seine to the Atlantic.

The second type of fortification is the cliff castle of the "Castel Coz" series. These were refuges rather than occupied sites for the sea-faring Celts of the northern coastal regions. The refuges were on headlands protected by the sea and by one, two, or three lines of bank-and-ditch. Kercaradec (2) is such a site. They are related to sites on the coast of Great Britain by trade goods and general topographic similarities; sites on both sides of the channel were those of small, mobile groups of sea-folk with limited agriculture. The third type of enceinte is so-called Belgic earthworks of the "Fécamp" series. Artifacts recovered from such sites—the Camp du Canada (4), for example—resemble the Dutch Hallstatt, of the Urnfield Tradition, and suggest a construction and occupation earlier than sites of the other two types, perhaps as a response to the incursions of the Cimbri and Teutones in 113-101 B.C. Instead of a murus gallicus, there are Fécamp ramparts. Wheeler and Richardson associated this feature with the Belgic ethnic group, not to be found outside Belgic territory. However, Ian Ralston of the University of Edinburgh (personal communication, 1971) has discovered, from survey work and through analysis of pertinent regional literature, seven examples of Fécamp ramparts well outside the area considered Belgica: Le Camp de Châteloy (17); Le Châtelier les Pornins (18); Les Fossés Sarrasins (15), which has yielded a "Fécamp" rampart with a burned murus gallicus beneath; Le Camp de Chou (13); Le Camp de César (12); Les Monts (10), which is probably Noviodunum; and finally Millançay (11).

Le Camp d'Artus (1) is a large tribal oppidum of the Osismii, a good example of the "Petit Celland" series (Fig. 14). The main gate was overthrown shortly after its construction: it has a single occupation level, a uniformity of ceramic types, and a single Gaulish coin of the tribe Osismii firmly attributable to the first half of the first century B.C. This is consistent with the date for the ceramics, which compares closely with ceramics from Le Châtellier (3), Kercaradec (2), Gergovia (21), and Bibracte (38). Other parallels with artifacts from Bibracte are in the metal objects recovered. The huge site apparently afforded safety for a large population, with or without their cattle, around 56 B.C. Le Camp d'Artus is a barren area agriculturally, and unlike Bibracte is not situated well enough to have been more than the initial point of trade in crude silver and lead; its size is therefore attributable to military or political, rather than economic, causes.

At Kercaradec (2), a site of the "Castel Coz" series, a pit covered with stone slabs and containing several thousand slingstones was reported by a local farmer. It is unlikely that ceramics recovered in Wheeler and Richardson's excavations are earlier than the first century B.C. They are of the "Ultimate Hallstatt" type, exhibiting features of Hallstatt and La Tène traditions combined in a provincial complex. This prolonged Hallstatt influence in a remote region reached spasmodically and imperfectly by developed La Tène cultures has also been seen at Gergovia (21), and other sites in southwestern France, as well as the south coastal site of Ensérune.

Wheeler and Richardson extensively excavated Le Châtellier (3), another site of the "Petit Celland" series. Slightly smaller than Camp d'Artus, Le Châtellier is surrounded by equally poor farm land interspersed with scrub, and there are no useful ores in the vicinity. The coalescence of population at this spot (which is relatively strategic) would only be under conditions of exceptional compulsion. The gates were destroyed by fire, and the work left unfinished. Excavation yielded an occupation level, not long or intensively settled, followed by a destruction level. Nineteen Gaulish coins ascribed to 56 B.C. were recovered; they had apparently circulated outside the boundaries of the issuing tribe, as they had been tested (bitten?) for intrinsic worth. Le Châtellier was another product of organized Gaulish resistance to Caesar in 56 B.C. It may also have been the rallying point for a composite force of a number of adjacent tribes led by Viridovix (chief of the Unelli, or Venelli).

Le Camp du Canada (4) was not a permanently occupied oppidum; a slight occupation followed construction and there was intermittent occupation

APPENDIX II

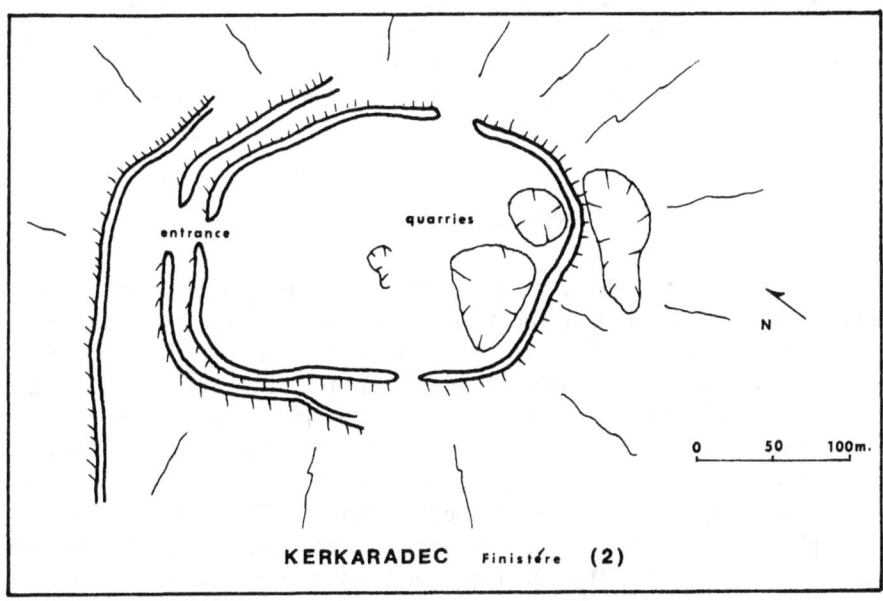

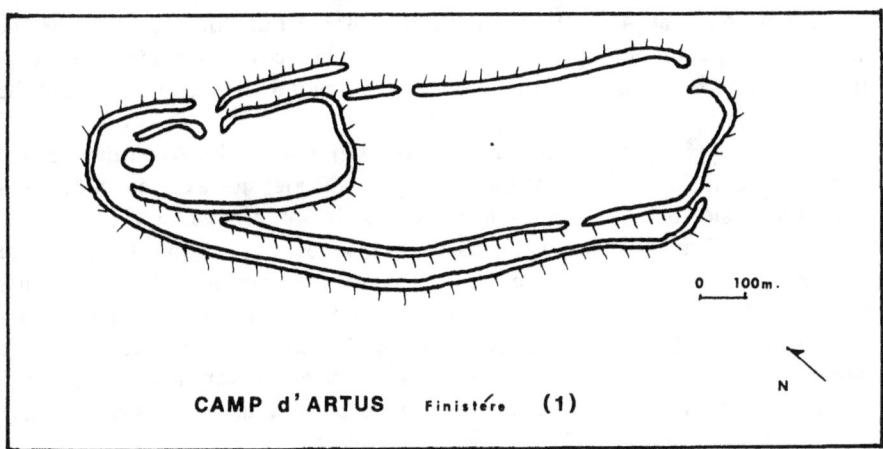

Fig. 14. Maps of Excavations at Kerkaradec (2) Finistère and Le Camp d' Artus (1) Finistère.

into the first century A.D. The camp itself cannot be later than the conquest of the region by Julius Caesar in 56-51 B.C. Le Camp du Canada is interesting in that it continued to be occupied a half century or more after the conquest, as were sites of Le Crêt Châtelard (42), Essalois (41), Murcens (26), l'Impernal (25), Bibracte (38), Villejoubert (20), and the oppidum of Joeuvres (39).

WEST-CENTRAL SITES

A number of small fortified sites have been reported, but it is difficult to obtain much more data than the approximate period and the mode of construction of the ramparts. Les Monts (10), Millançay (11), Camp de César (12), Camp de Chou (13), Les Fossés Sarrasins (15), Camp de Châteloy (17), and Le Châtelier les Pornins (18) are such sites. They are apparently contemporaneous, around the time of Caesar's conquest, and all share as well the interesting feature of having Fécamp ramparts well outside the Belgic ethnic area. Nearby Avaricum (16), however, beneath modern Bourges (Cher), contains a classic example of the murus gallicus. Avaricum is mentioned in the *Commentaries* (*BG*, 7, 13-15; 17; 22-23) as the largest and best fortified town in the territory of the Bituriges, situated in a most fertile district. Grenier (1945) suggests its population stood at 40,000. It has been explored but not excavated, as the modern town, a bustling provincial capitol, all but covers the site. The Celtic strata lie 15 m beneath the cathedral and 8 m beyond the modern limits of the city.

Gergovia (21), near modern Clermont-Ferrand, is the Arvernian stronghold Vercingetorix held against Caesar (Fig. 15). Extensive excavation has produced two major occupational layers: the first is Bronze Age, and lies beneath the site's fortifications. The fortifications themselves date to about the period of conquest, but there is no trace of contemporary occupation. This suggests that the impetus for erecting the defenses may have been the Roman invasion of Gaul. This parallels oppida in Normandy and Brittany; such fortifications were apparently used by scattered tribesmen as a refuge but were not continuously occupied at the time. The fortifications were constructed of locally abundant stone, without timbers, as the area was probably as sparsely wooded as it is today. The enclosed area was 70-75 hectares (1 hectare = 2.471 acres). The major occupation of the site took place beginning immediately after the Roman conquest and included a number of Roman elements. Houses like those in the Parc aux Chevaux at Bibracte were found, but with more of a Roman than a Gallic character. There was a market area and a metalworking quarter, also resembling Bibracte, and the ceramics were comparable. The site continued to be occupied through the Claudian period, and was subsequently razed.

APPENDIX II

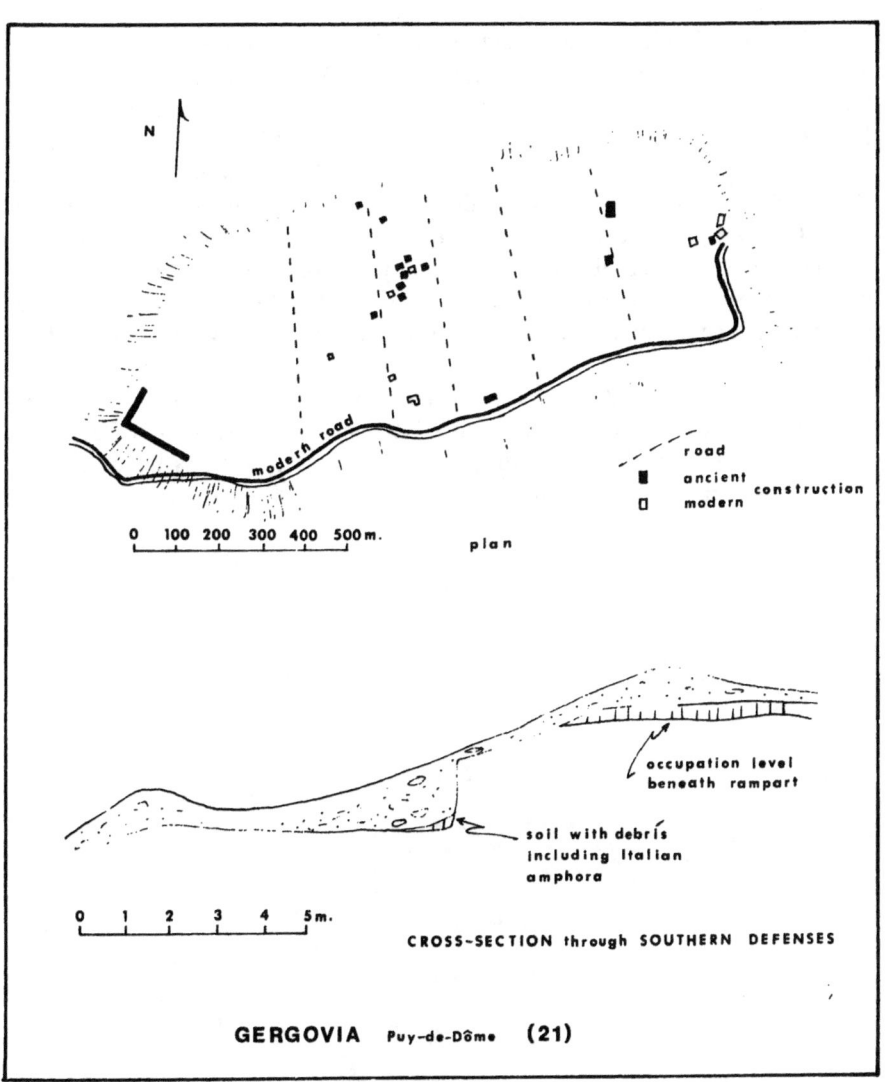

Fig. 15. Map of Excavations at Gergovia (21) Puy-de-Dôme.

SOUTHWESTERN SITES

Le Puy d'Issolu (24) is thought on the basis of linguistic and archaeological evidence to have been Uxellodunum, the city of Drappes and Lucterius (Fig. 16). When in 1860 a commission was set up to ascertain the location of Uxellodunum (Fig. 17), excavations were undertaken at l'Impernal (25) and for some time the prevailing opinion was that l'Impernal was Uxellodunum. There are still those who support this view or the position that Murcens (26) is the site (Fig. 18), but most recent investigators favor le Puy d'Issolu. Castagne (1874) thought that l'Impernal was of secondary importance to Murcens and Puy d'Issolu and was designed to serve as a refuge for a limited population. It was occupied for some time after the conquest and the entire plateau yielded Gallo-Roman remains.

Murcens is thought to have existed somewhat before Caesar's time, built as a response to either the founding of *Provincia Romana* in 121 B.C., or the attacks of the Cimbri and Teutones in 110 B.C. Excavations uncovered what had been an active industrial quarter.

APPENDIX II 93

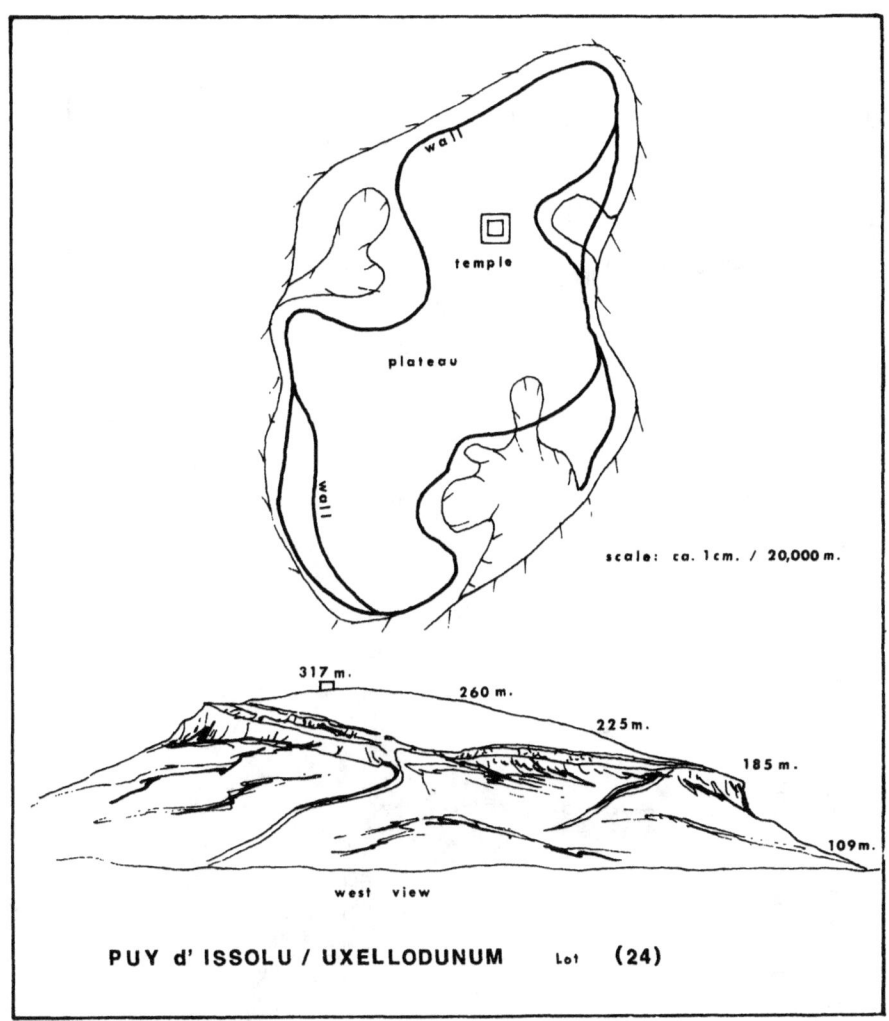

Fig. 16. Map of Excavations at Puy-d' Issolu/Uxellodunum (24).

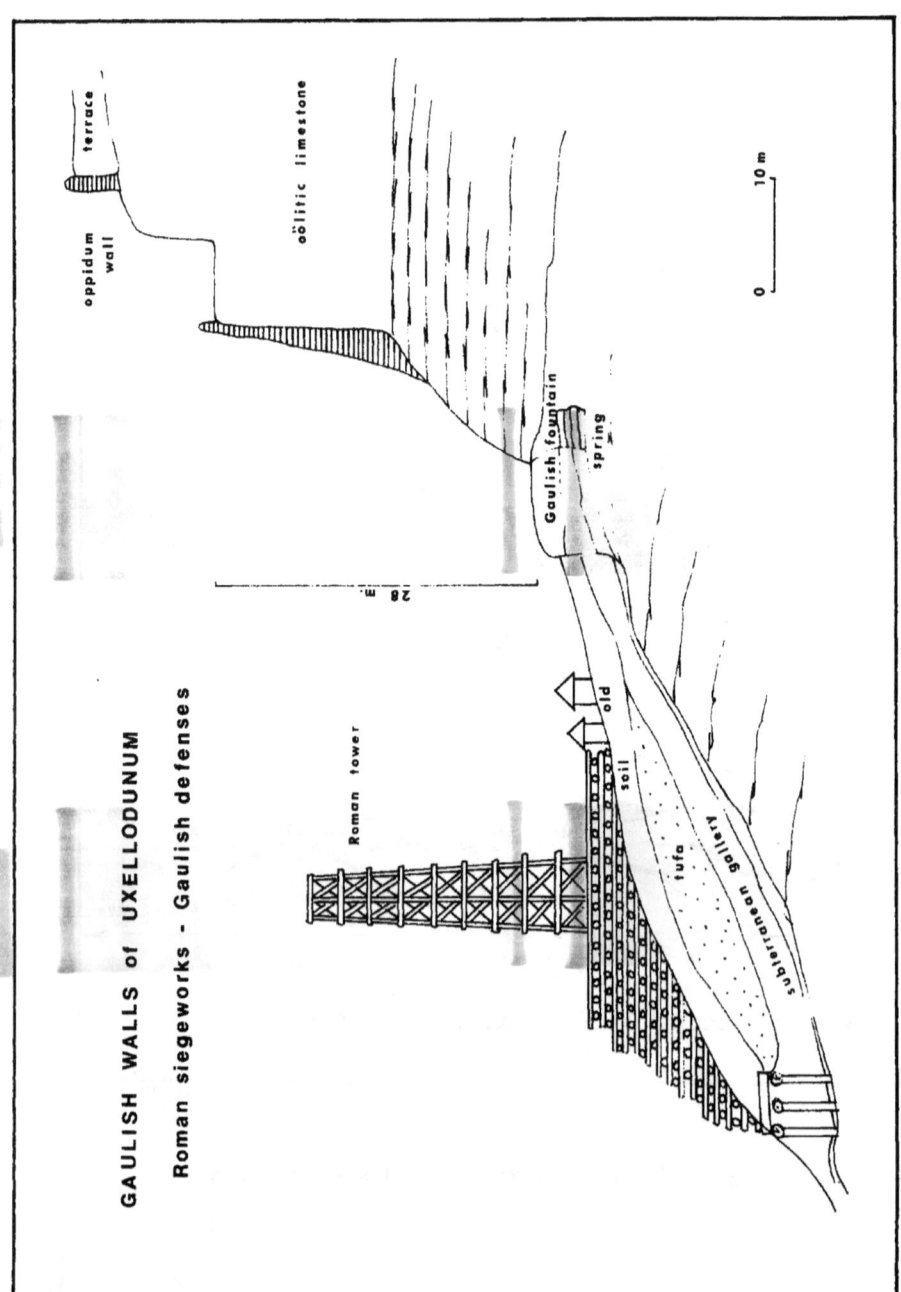

Fig. 17. Gaulish Walls of Uxellodunum (Roman Seigeworks; Gaulish Defenses).

APPENDIX II

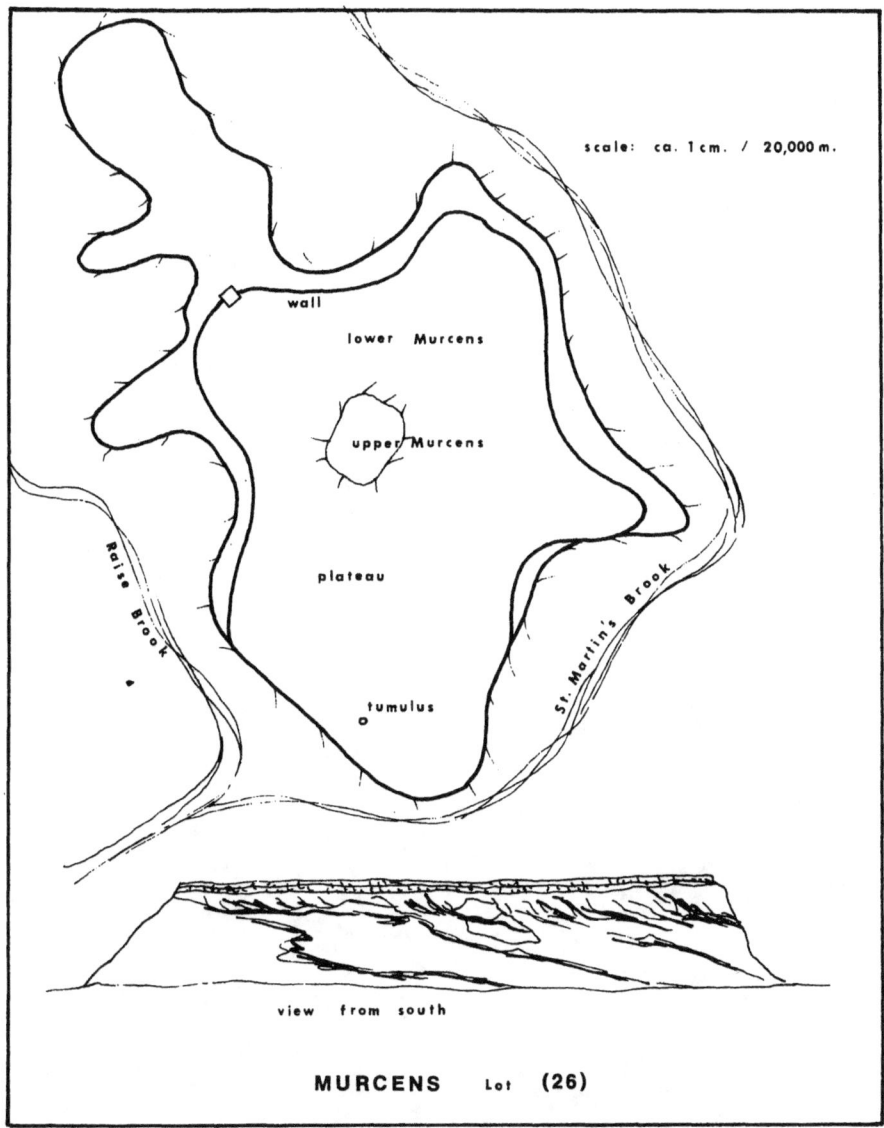

Fig. 18. Map of Excavations at Murcens (26).

APPENDIX III

SITE DATA TABLES

TABLE 1

NORTH COASTAL SITES

Name of Site	Camp d'Artus	Kercaradec	Le Châtellier	Camp du Canada	Câtelier	Camp de la Ségourie	Camp du Câstellier	LaBurette	Poulailler
Commune	Huelgoat	Penhars	Le Petit Celland	Fécamp	Duclair	Fief-Sauvin	Saint-Désir	Banville	Landéan
Department	Finistère	Finistère	Manche	Seine-Atlantique	Seine-Atlantique	Maine-et-Loire	Calvados	Calvados	Ille-et-Vilaine
Nearby Water Source									
(a) near river or stream	–	+	–	+	+	+	–	+	+
(b) near sea	+	+	+	+	+	–	+	+	–
(c) near springs, lake	–	–	–	–	–	–	–	–	–
Relief									
(a) hillfort or promontory fort	+	+	+	+	+	+	+	+	+
(b) fortified, but low-lying	–	–	–	–	–	–	–	–	–
Advantages of Location									
(a) political	–	–	+	+	+	+	–	+	+
(b) agricultural	–	–	–	–	+	+	–	–	–
(c) commercial	+	–	–	+	+	+	–	+	–
Affiliations									
(a) with other sites	2, 3 19 24	24 43	1	19 20 22-3, 37, 41					
(b) ethnic	Osismii	Venetes	Unelli	Caletes	Belgic Veliocasses	Andes	Lexovii	Lexovii	Ambibarii

99

Table 1 cont'd

Name of Site	Camp d'Artus	Kercaradec	Le Chatellier	Camp du Canada	Catelier	Camp de la Ségourie	Camp du Castellier	LaBurette	Poulailler
Occupation									
(a) type									
(1) intermittent	–	–	+	+	–	NI	+	NI	–
(2) extended	–	–	–	–	–		–		–
(3) brief	+	+	+	–	+		+		+
(b) date									
(1) single occ'n La Tène III	+	+	+	–	+	–	+	NI	+
(2) La Tène, not post-conquest	–	–	–	–	–	–	–		–
(3) La Tène and post-conquest	–	–	–	+	–	+	–		–
(c) fortification type									
(1) murus gallicus	–	–	–	–	–	+	+	+?	–
(2) Fécamp	+	+	+	+	+	–	–	–	+
(3) other	–	–	–	–	–	–	–	–	–
(d) size (in acres)	75.0	5.5	48.0	50.0	24.5	NI	390.0	5.5	46.0

TABLE 2
WEST-CENTRAL SITE

Name of Site	Les Monts	Millançay	Camp de César	Camp de Chou	Camp de César	Les Fossés Sarrasins	Avaricum	Camp de Châteloy	Le Châtelier les Pornins	Camp de Cornouin	Villejoubert	Gergovia	Camp de Corny
Commune	Neung-sur-Beuvron	Romorantin	Sidiailles	Moulins-sur-Yèvre	La Groutte	Châteaumeillant	Bourges	Hérrison	Luant	Lussac-les-Châteaux	St.-Denis-des-Murs	Puy-de-Dôme	Meunet-Planches
Department	Loir-et-Cher	Loir-et-Cher	Cher	Cher	Cher	Cher	Cher	Allier	Indre	Vienne	Haute-Vienne	Puy-de-Dôme	Indre
Nearby Water Source													
(a) near river or stream	+	−	+	+	+	−	+	+	+	+	+	+	+
(b) near sea	−	−	−	−	−	−	−	−	−	−	−	−	−
(c) near springs, lake	−	+	−	−	−	−	+	−	−	−	−	−	−
Relief													
(a) hillfort or promontory fort	−	−	+	−	−	−	−	+	+	+	+	+	+
(b) fortified, but low-lying	+	+	−	+	+	+	+	−	−	−	−	−	−
Advantages of Location													
(a) political	−	+	+	+	+	+	+	+	+	+	+	+	+
(b) agricultural	+	+	−	−	+	+	+	−	−	+	+	+	−
(c) commercial	+	+	−	−	+	+	+	+	+	+	+	+	−

Table 2 cont'd

Name of Site	Les Monts	Millan-cay	Camp de César	Camp de Chou	Camp de César	Les Fossés Sarrasins	Avari-cum	Camp de Chateloy	Le Chatelier les Pornins	Camp de Cornouin	Villejou-bert	Ger-govia	Camp de Corny
Affiliations													
(a) with other sites	27, 30, 33-4	26, 29	34, 31	26-30	33-34						18, 19; 41-2; 38	19	
(b) ethnic	Bituri-ges	Bituri-ges	Bituri-ges	Bituri-ges	Bituri-ges	Bituri-ges	Bituri-ges	Bituri-ges	Bituri-ges	Pictones	Lemo-vices	Arver-ni	Bituriges
Occupation													
(a) type													
(1) intermittent	NI	NI	−	−	NI	−	−	NI	NI	NI	+	+	NI
(2) extended			+	−		+	+				−	−	
(3) brief			−	+		−	−				−	−	
(b) date													
(1) single occ'n La Tène III	NI	−	(?)+	−	NI	−	−	NI	NI	NI	−	−	−
(2) La Tène, not post-conquest		+	−	−		−	−				−	−	−
(3) La Tène and post-conquest		−	−	+		+	+				+	+	+
(c) fortification type													
(1) murus gallicus	−	−	early? +	−	early +	early +	+	early +	−	+	+	−	+
(2) Fécamp	+	+ later	−	+	+ later	+ later	−	+	+	−	−	−	−
(3) other	−	−	−	−	−	−	−	−	−	−	−	−	−
(d) size (in acres)	25.0	12.5	32.5	40.0	NI	50.0	NI	NI	10.0	25.0	NI	175.0	2.5

APPENDIX III

TABLE 3

SOUTHWESTERN SITES

Name of Site	Camp de Périgueux	Puy d' Issolu	l'Impernal (UXELLODUNUM)	Murcens	Puy du Tour
Commune	Coulounie	–	Luzech	Cras	Monceaux
Department	Dordogne	Lot	Lot	Lot	Corrèze
Nearby Water Sources					
(a) near river or stream	+	+	+	+	+
(b) near sea	–	–	–	–	–
(c) near springs, lake	–	+	–	–	–
Relief					
(a) hillfort or promontory fort	+	+	+	+	+
(b) fortified, but low-lying	–	–	–	–	–
Advantages of Location					
(a) political	–	+	–	+	+
(b) agricultural	+	+	+	+	+
(c) commercial	–	+	–	+	+
Affiliations					
(a) with other sites		42		40	37
(b) ethnic	Petrocorii	Cadurci	Cadurci	Cadurci	Lemovices
Occupation					
(a) type	NI				
(1) intermittent		–	+	–	–
(2) extended		+	–	+	+
(3) brief		–	–	–	–
(b) date	NI				
(1) single occ'n La Tène III		–	–	–	–
(2) La Tène, not post-conquest		–	–	–	+
(3) La Tène and post-conquest		+	+	+	–
(c) fortification type					
(1) murus gallicus	+	–	+	+	+
(2) Fécamp	–	–	–	–	–
(3) other	–	+	–	–	–
(d) size (in acres)	NI	250.0	40.0	250.0	NI

TABLE 4

SOUTH COASTAL SITES

Name of Site	Ensérune	Glanum	Entremont
Commune	Béziers	St.-Rémy-de-Provence	Aix-en Provence
Department	Hérault	Bouches-du Rhône	Bouches-du-Rhône
Nearby Water Source			
(a) near river or stream	+	+	+
(b) near sea	+	+	+
(c) near springs, lake	+	−	+
Relief			
(a) hillfort or promontory fort	+	+	+
(b) fortified but low-lying	−	−	−
Advantages of Location			
(a) political	+	+	+
(b) agricultural	+	+	+
(c) commercial	+	+	+
Affiliations			
(a) with other sites	Volcae Tectosages	Saluvii	Commoni
(b) ethnic			
Occupation			
(a) type			
(1) intermittent	−	−	−
(2) extended	+	+	+
(3) brief	−	−	−
(b) date			
(1) single occ'n, La Tène III	−	−	−
(2) La Tène, not post-conquest	−	−	+
(3) La Tène, and post-conquest	+	+	−
(c) fortification type			
(1) murus gallicus	−	−	−
(2) Fécamp	−	−	−
(3) other	+	+	+ (so-called Cyclopean)
(d) size (in acres)	NI	NI	NI

APPENDIX III

TABLE 5
RHÔNE CORRIDOR

Name of Site	Pommiers (Noviodunum)	Le Châtelet	Le Câtelet	Mont Châtel	Vertault	Laignes	Mont Lassois	Mont Auxois (Alesia)	Bibracte	Joeuvres	Châtelard de Chazi	Essalois	Crêt Châtelard	Ste.-Blandine
Commune	Soissons	Montigny-sur-Engrain	Avesnelles	Bovioles	Vertault	Vix		Alise-Ste.-Reine	St-Léger-Sous-Beuvray	St. Maurice-sur-Loire	St-Georges-de-Baroille	Chambles	St-Marcel-des-Félines	Vienne
Department	Aisne	Aisne	Nord	Meuse	Côte-d'Or	Côte-d'Or	Côte-d'Or	Côte-d'Or	Saône-et-Loire/Nièvre	Loire	Loire	Loire	Loire	Vienne
Nearby Water Source														
(a) near river or stream	+	+	+	+	+	+	+	+	+	+	+	+	+	+
(b) near sea	−	−	−	−	−	−	−	−	−	−	−	−	−	−
(c) near springs, lake	−	−	−	−	−	−	−	−	+	−	−	−	−	−
Relief														
(a) hillfort or promontory fort	+	+	+	+	+	+	+	+	+	+	+	+	+	+
(b) fortified but low-lying	−	−	−	−	−	−	−	−	−	−	−	−	−	−
Advantages of Location														
(a) political	+	+	+	+	+	+	+	+	+	+	+	+	+	+
(b) agricultural	+	+	+	+	+	+	+	+	+	+	+	+	+	+
(c) commercial	+	+	+	+	+	+	+	+	+	+	+	+	+	+

Table 5 cont'd

Name of Site	Pommiers (Noviodunum)	Le Châtelet	Le Chatelet Chatel	Mont Châtel	Vertault	Mont Lassois	Mont Auxois (Alesia)	Bibracte	Joeuvres	Châtelard de Chazi	Essalois	Crêt Chatelard	Ste.-Blandine
Affiliations													
(a) with other sites								22, 23				29	29
(b) ethnic	Suessiones	Suessiones	Nervii	Leuci	Lingones	Lingones	Mandubii	Aedui	Segusiavi	Segusiavi	Segusiavi	Segusiavi	Allobroges
(b) date		NI								NI			
(1) single occ'n La Tène III	–	–	–	–	–	–	–	–	–	–	–	–	–
(2) La Tène, not post-conq.	+	–	–	–	–	–	–	–	–	–	–	–	–
(3) La Tène & post-conq.	–	+	+	+	+	+	+	+	+	+	+	+	+
(c) fortification type													
(1) murus gallicus	–	+	+ early	+	+	+	+	+	–	+	+	–	–
(2) Fécamp	+	–	+ later	–	–	–	–	–	–	–	–	–	–
(3) other	–	–	–	–	–	–	–	–	+	+	+	–	+
(d) size (in acres)	100.0	22.5	NI	125.0	NI	10.0	242.5	337.5	188.0	19.0	NI	62.5	NI

BIBLIOGRAPHY

A. CLASSICAL AUTHORS
(translations are Loeb Classical Library unless otherwise noted)

Ammianus Marcellinus (325/30-395 A.D.), *Historia*
    translated by J. C. Rolfe

Athenaeus, *Deinosophistai (The Learned at Dinner)*
    translated by C. B. Gulick

Julius Caesar, *De Bello Gallico*
    translated by H. J. Edwards, Caesar, *The Gallic War,* London. John Warrington, *Caesar's War Commentaries,* New York, Dutton & Company, 1958.

Cyril of Alexandria, *Opera*
    translated by P. E. Pusey, 7 vols., Oxford 1868-77

Dio Chrysostom (c. 40-120 A.D.), *Opera*
    translated by J. W. Cohoon, H. L. Crosby

Diodorus Siculus (fl. 60-30 B.C.), *Bibliotheke (Library of History)*
    translated by C. H. Oldfather

Diogenes Laertius (fl. ca. 240 A.D.), *Lives of the Philosophers*
    translated by R. D. Hicks

Lucan (39-65 A.D.), *Pharsalia, De Bello Civili*
    translated by J. D. Duff

Plutarch (A.D. 45-ca. 120 A.D.), *Vitae*
    edited and revised by Arthur Hugh Clough, (1864).
    Everyman's Library, in 3 vols., 1910.

Polybius (ca. 200-after 118 B.C.), *Historia*
    translated by Evelyn S. Shuckburgh *The Histories,* in 2 vols. from a text by F. Hultsch, Indiana University Press.

Strabo (c. 63-B.C.–21 A.D.), *Geographia* (esp. book IV)

Tacitus (ca. 56-after 113 A.D.) *The Histories; Annals*
    translated by M. Hutton, C. H. Moore, J. Jackson
    translated by Alfred J. Church and W. J. Hutton (London, MacMillan & Co. Ltd.)

Oxford Classical Dictionary
    ed. by N. G. L. Hammond and H. H. Scullard, 2nd edition 1970, Oxford, the Clarendon Press.

B. SITE BIBLIOGRAPHY

Site Number

Benoit, Ferdinand
    1957 *Entremont,* Aix-en-Provence.   30
    "Résultats historiques des fouilles d'Entremont" dans *Gallia* V, 1 (1948) 81-98; VI, 1 (1948) 213; VII (1950) 117-119, 125; XI, 1 (1953) 106-107; XII, 2 (1954) 285-94; XIV, 2 (1956) 218-222; XVI, 2 (1958) 412-415; XVIII, 2 (1960) 291-94; XX, 2 (1962) 689-692; XXII (1964) 573; XXVI (1968) 1-32.   30

Brogan, Olwen and E. Desforges
    1940 "Gergovia," *Archaeological Journal* 97, (1940) p 1-36.   21

Bulliot, J. G.
    1870 *Ann. du l'Institut des Provinces des Sociétés Savantes et des Congrès Sci.* XII (2e ser.) p. 164-66.   38
    1899 *Fouilles de Mont Beuvray de 1867 à 1895,* 2 vols. Autun.   38
    Mémoires de la Société Eduenne, vols. 1 (1872); 2 (1873); 4 (1875); 5 (1876); 8 (1879); 10 (1881); 12 (1883); 13 (1884); 14 (1885); 16 (1888); 23 (1895); 24 (1896); 27 (1899); 32 (1904).   38

Caesar, Gaius Julius
    De Bello Gallico   15, 21, 37, 38

Castagné, M.
    1874 Mem. sur les ouvrages de fortification des oppidums gaulois de Murcesis, d'Uxellodunum et de l'Impernal (Luzech) situes dans le département du Lot, in *Congrès Archéologique de France* (Agen et Toulouse) 1874, pp. 427-538.   24, 25, 26

Chapotat, Gabriel
    1970 Vienne Gauloise: le matériel de La Tène III trouvé sur la colline de Ste.-Blandine, 2 vols., Lyon, 1971 (publ. du Centre des Etudes rom. et gallo-rom.).   43

Site Number

Déchelette, Joseph
    1900 Note Sur l'oppidum de Bibracte et les principales stations gauloises contemporaines. 12e sess., Paris p. 418-27, *Congrès Internationaux d'Anthropologie et d'Archéologie Préhistorique*: Comptes rendus des congrès, Masson: Paris   38
    1903 *L'Oppidum de Bibracte,* Paris.   38
    1904 *Les Fouilles du Mont Beuvray de 1897-1901,* Autun.   38
    1927 (et 1913) Manuel d'Archéologie Préhistorique, Celtique et Gallo-Romaine, in 4 vols., esp. vol. IV.   6, 32, 33, 34, 35, 39, 40, 41, 42

Durand, P.
    1899- "le Crêt Châtelard," *Diana* XI (1899-1900)   42
    1900

Espérandieu, E.
    1908 *Les Fouilles d'Alesia de 1906.*   37

Eydoux, H. P.
    1958 Monuments et Trésors de la Gaule, *Entremont.*   30

Hugoniot, E. et J. Gourvest
    1961 L'Oppidum de Mediolanum, Chateaumeillant (Cher) Campagnes de fouille 1956-1960, in *Celticum,* supp. à Ogam-Trad'n Celtique no. 73-75, 1961, pp. 193-204.   15

Hogg, A. H. A.
    1969 "A Sample of French Hill-Forts," *Antiquity* XLIII, p. 260-73.   24, 26

Jannoray, Jean
    1955 *Ensérune: Contributions a l'Etude des civilizations pre-Romains de la Gaule Méridionale.* 2 vols. publiée par Bibliothèque des Ecoles Françaises d'Athènes et de Rome, Paris no. 181.   28
           Gallia. "Fouilles de Ensérune" I (1943) 5-14; IV (1946) 357-60; VI, 1 (1948) 203-06; VIII (1950) 112-115; XI, 1 (1953) 96-99; XII, 2 (1954); XIV, 2 (1956) 210-16; XVII, 2 (1959) 462.   28

Joffroy, René
    1953 "La Station Hallstattienne du Mont Lassois" *Rev. Arch. de l'Est et du Centre-Est* IV, p. 97-107.   36
    1954 *Le Trésor de Vix,* Presse Universitaire de France.   36

La Baume, P. and B. F. Fournier
    1962 *Gergovie,* Clermont-Ferrand.   21

Site Number

Labrousse, M.
1966 Au dossier d'Uxellodunum, in *Mélanges d'Archéologie d'Epigraphie et d'Histoire offerts a Jérome Carcopino* Paris, Hachette, pp. 563-583. 24

Lassus, J., A. Grenier and J. J. Hatt
"Fouilles de Gergovia in *Gallia* I, 2 (1943) p. 71-124; V, 2 (1947) p. 271-300; VI, 1 (1948) p. 31-95; VIII (1950) p. 14-53. 21

Le Gall, Joel
1963 *Alésia: Archéologie et Histoire*, Résurrection du Passé, Fayard, Paris. 37

Lucas-Shadwell, N. and Olwen Brogan
1936 "Gergovia," *Antiquity* 10 (1936), p. 210-17. 21

Murat, Auguste
1962 A propos de la période de La Tène III apports récents de la station du Puy du Tour, *Ogam-tradition* celtique XIX, fasc. 1, Jan.-Mar. 1962. 27

Noëlas, Frédéric
1885 De l'emplacement des villes gallo-romaines Mediolanum, Forum Segusiavorum, etc. 52e sess., Montbrison, 190 (1885), *Congrès* Archéologique de France, Comptes Rendus des congrès annuels de la Société francaise d'Archéologie, Caen. 15

Périchon, Robert
1961 "Note Préliminaire sur les recherches à l'oppidum de Joeuvre (Loire)" *Celticum-Ogam tradition celtique* no. 73-75, p. 205-212, Rennes. 39

Preynat, Jean-Paul
1962 "Un site de La Tène en Forez: l'oppidum de Essalois" in: *Ogam-tradition celtique* XIV, fasc. 2-3 (April-June), p. 287-314.

Renaud, Jean
1962 "Notes sur l'oppidum d'Essalois (Loire)" *Ogam-tradition celtique* XIV, fasc. 1, p. 57-67. 41

Rolland, H.
1968 "Glanum" dans *Revue Archéologique de Narbonnaise* 1 (1968), p. 93-99. 29
"Fouilles de Glanum" in *Gallia* I, 2 (1943) 207-228; II (1944) 167-223; VI, 1 (1948) 141-169; VII (1950) 131-32; XI, 1 (1953) 3-17; XII, 2 (1954) 448-51; XIV, 2 (1956) 241-46; XVI, 1 (1958) 95-114; XXI (1963) 111-124, 307; XXII (1964) 1-24; XXV (1967) 407; suppléments I, (1946); XI (1958).

Site Number

Toutain, J.
   1943 *40 Années de fouilles à Alésia* REA 1943, p. 628-40   37

Vauvillé, Octave
   1887 "Découvertes faites dans l'opidum de Pommiers," *Congrès archéologique de France*,
   1894 "Le Camp de Pommiers," *Bull. de la Société d'Anthropologie de Paris*, p. 258.   31

Ward Perkins, J. B.
   1940-41 "The Pottery at Gergovia," *Antiquity Journal*, 1940-1.   21

Wernert, Paul
   1949 "Mont Lassois, Cote-d'Or," *Gallia* VII, p. 247-50.   36

Wheeler, R. E. M.
   1939 "Iron-Age Camps in Northwest France and Southwest Britain," *Antiquity* XIII, p. 69.   9

Wheeler, R. E. M. and Katherine M. Richardson
   1957 *Hill Forts of Northern France*. Reports of the Research Committee of the Society of Antiquaries of London, no. XIX, Oxford.   1-9, 16, 19-20, 23, 25-27, 31-42

C. MODERN WORKS CONSULTED

   1865 Dictionnaire archélogique de la Gaule époque celtique publié par la commission instituée au Ministère de l'Instruction Publique et des Beaux Arts. Tome premier A-G. MDCCCLXV, Paris, Imprimerie Nationale.

   1969 *Recherches sur les structures sociales dans l'antiquité classique*. Caen, 25-26 Avril, 1969. Colloques nationaux du Centre national de la recherche scientifique, sciences humaines.

d'Arbois de Jubainville, H.
   1883 Cours de litterature celtique, 12 vol., Paris, especially vols. I (1883); IV
   1899 (1899).
   1895 *Études sur le droit celtique*, Paris.

Colbert de Beaulieu, J. B.
   1964-65 Notes d'épigraphie monétaire gauloise (IV). *Etudes Celtiques* XI, 1, pp. 46-69.

Bengtson, Hermann and Vladimir Milojčić
   1954 *Grosser Historischer Weltatlas*, Munich.

Benoit, Ferdinand
    1965 *Recherches sur l'hèllenisation du midi de la Gaule* (Aix)

Binchy, D. A. (ed).
    1936 *Studies in Early Irish Law*. Royal Irish Academy, Dublin.

Blanchet, Adrien
    1905 *Traité des Monnaies Gauloises*. 2 vols. Paris.

Blanchet, A.
    1931 *Carte Archéologique Gallo-Romaine*. Hachette et Cie, Paris.

Brown, T. S.
    1958 *Timaeus of Taurominium*. University of California Press.

Büchsenschutz, Oliver
    1971 "État de la Rechérche sur les Oppida en France, particulièrement dans le Centre," *Archeologické Rozhledy* XXIII, p. 406-416.

Buhot de Kersers, A.
    1868 Les Enceintes en terre dans le département du Cher, *Men. Soc. Ant. du Centre* i, 15 and 43-46.

Bulliot, J-G et Henry de Fontenay
    1875 *L'Art de l'Emaillerie Chez les Eduens avant l'ère Chrétienne*. Paris, Champion.

Bulliot, J-G et J. Roidot
    1879 *Cité Gauloise* selon l'histoire et les traditions. Autun.

Bunbury, E. H.
    1879 *A History of Ancient Geography*, vol. II, London, John Murry.

Chadwick, Nora
    1966 *The Druids*. University of Wales Press, Cardiff.

Chorley, Richard J. and Peter Haggett
    1967 *Socio-Economic Models in Geography*. Methuen, London.

Cole, Thomas
    1967 *Democritus and the Sources of Greek Anthropology*. American Philological Association Monograph 25, Western Reserve University Press.

Davies, Oliver
    1935 *Roman Mines in Europe*. Oxford, Clarendon Press.

Déchelette, Joseph
    1903 *L'Oppidum de Bibracte*.
    1913 *Manuel d'Archéologie Préhistorique et Gallo-Romaine*, no. 2, Vol. II, "Archéologie Celtique ou Protohistorique," Paris, Picard.

BIBLIOGRAPHY

DeLaet, S. J.
    1964 "Romans, Celts, and Germans in Northern Gaul," *Diogenes*, 47, 83-101.

Desjardins, Ernest
    1885 *Géographie de la Gaule Romaine*, tomes 2 & 3, Paris Librairie Hachette et Cie.

DeWitt, Norman
    1935 *Urbanization and Franchise in Roman Gaul*. Ph.D. dissertation, Johns Hopkins University.
    1938 "The Druids and Romanization" in: *Trn. & Proc. of Am. Phil. Ass'n.* LXIX, p. 319.

Dodds, E. R.
    1968 *The Greeks and the Irrational*. University of California Press, Berkeley and L.A., first printing 1951.

Drda, Petr *et al.*
    1971 "Oppida un Viereckschanzen" *Archeologické Rozhledy*, XXIII, p. 288-91.

Dubois, Marcel
    1891 *Examen de la Géographie de Strabon*, étude critique de la méthode et des sources, Paris.

Edelstein, Ludwig
    1967 *The Idea of Progress in Classical Antiquity*. John Hopkins Press, Baltimore.

Fallers, Lloyd A.
    1966 "A Note on the Trickle Effect" in: Reinhard Bendix and Seymour Martin Lipset, eds., *Status, Class and Power*, p. 402-5.

Faucher, D. *et al.*
    1951- *La France:* géographie-tourisme. Larousse, 2 vols.
    1952

Frank, T.
    1914 Roman Imperialism, New York.

Fustel de Coulanges, Numa Denis
    1908 *Histoire des Institutions Politiques de l'Ancienne France: La Gaule Romaine*. Paris, Libraire Hachette et cie.

Grenier, Albert
    1945 *Les Gaulois*. Payot, Paris.

Haggett, Peter
    1966 *Locational Analysis in Human Geography*. St. Martin's Press, NYC.

Hatt, J. J.
    1966 *Histoire de la Gaule Romaine* (120 av. J-C-451 a J-C). Payot, Paris.

Hatt, J. J. (cont'd)
    1970 *Les Celtes et les Gallo-Romains.* Archaeologia Mundi, Editions Nagel, Genéve.

Havelock, Eric A.
    1957 *The Liberal Temper in Greek Politics.* Yale University Press, New Haven and London.

Holmes, T. Rice
    1911 *Caesar's Conquest of Gaul.* Oxford.

Hubert, Henri
    1950 *Les Celtes depuis l'époque de La Tène et la civilisation celtique.* Paris.

Jacobsthal,
    Early Celtic Art. Oxford.

de Jonge, P.
    1953 *Philological and Historical Commentary on Ammianus Marcellinus.* Groningen.

Jullian, C.
    1908 *Histoire de la Gaule,* 8 vols., Paris 1908-26.

King, Leslie J.
    1969 *Statistical Analysis in Geography.* Prentice-Hall, N.J.

Last, Hugh
    1949 "Rome and the Druids—a Note" in: *Journal of Roman Studies,* 39, 1-5.

Lengyel, Lancelot
    1969 *Le Secret des Celtes.* Choisy-le-Roi, France ed. Robert Morel.

Lesky, Albin
    1966 *A History of Greek Literature,* first publsihed, 1957; English translation.

Lovejoy, A. O. & G. Boas
    1935 *Primitivism and Related Ideas in Antiquity.* Baltimore, John Hopkins Press.

Longnon, Auguste (Honore)
    1885 *Atlas Historique de la France depuis César jusqu'à nos jours.*

MacKendrick, Paul
    1971 *Roman Gaul.* St. Martin's Press.

Martonne, de E. A.
    1933 *Geographical Regions of France.* Heinemann, London.

Mattingly, H.
    1948 Notes in: *Tacitus on Britain and Germany,* a translation of the *Agricola and Germania.* Penguin Books, Middlesex.

Mauss, M.
    1926 "Sur un texte de Posidonius," *Revue Celtique*, XLI, p. 497.

Momigliano, Arnaldo
    1966 "The Place of Herodotus on the History of Historiography," in: *Studies in Historiography*, ch. 8, Harper and Row Publishers.

Mommsen, Theodor
    1886 *The Provinces of The Roman Empire: The European Provinces*. Selections from Hist. of Rome, V. 5, book 8, ed. 2/intro. by T. Robert S. Broughton, U. Chicago Press, Chicago and London.

Monkhouse, F. J.
    1967 *A Regional Geography of Western Europe*. Praeger, New York.

Moreau de Jonnes, Alexander
    1851 Statistique des Peuples de l'Antiquité. Tome II. Paris.

de la Noé, le Général
    1887 Principes de la fortification antique, depuis les temps préhistoriques jusqu'aux Croisades pour servir au classement des enceintes dont le sol de la France a conservé la trace. *Bulletin de Géographie Historique et Descriptive* (1887) Comité des Travaux Historiques et Scientifiques Leroux: Paris.

Nutting, Herbert C.
    1934 "Comments on Lucan," in: *University of California Publications*, Vol. XI (1930-33) nos. 3,4,5,8,9,10,11,&12.

Phillips, E. D.
    1964 "The Greek Vision of Prehistory," in: *Antiquity*, XXXVIII, p. 171-178. ed. by Glyn Daniel.

Piggott, Stuart
    1968 *The Druids*. Thames & Hudson, London.

Polanyi, Karl, Conrad Arensberg and Harry W. Pearson
    1957 *Trade and Market in the Early Empires*. Free Press, NYC.

Pounds, G. Norman
    1971 "The Urbanization of the Classical World." *Ekistics*, 182.

Powell, T. G. E.
    1958 *The Celts*. Thames and Hudson, London.

Rambaud, Michel
    1953 *L'art de la déformation historique dans les Commentaires de César*. Annales de l'Université de Lyon, troisième série, fase. 23. Lettres, Paris.

Renfrew, Colin
    1969 "Trade and Culture Process in European Prehistory" *Current Anthropology* 10:151-69.

Rowlett, Ralph
    1968 "The Iron Age North of the Alps" *Science* vol. 161, p. 123-34

Serrure, C. A.
    1885 *Etudes sur la Numismatique Gauloise.*

Service, Elman R.
    1972 *Profiles in Ethnology.* Harper and Row, NYC.

Sherwin-White, A. N.
    1939 *Roman Citizenship.* Oxford.

Silverman, Sydel
    1965 "Patronage and Community—National Relationships in Central Italy," *Ethnology*, Vol. IV, pp. 183-84.

Smith, C. T.
    1967 *An Historical Geography of Western Europe.* Longmans, Green & Co. London.

Thévenot, E.
    1949 *Histoire des Gaulois.* Collection *Que sais-je?* Paris.

Thompson, E. A.
    1947 *The Historical Work of Ammianus Marcellinus.* Cambridge University Press.

Tierney, J. J.
    1960 "The Celtic Ethnography of Posidonius," in: vol. 60, sec. C., paper 5, of *Proceedings of the Royal Irish Academy*, Dublin.

Tischler, O.
    1885 *Congrès Archéologique de France*, LXI (1885) p. 157.
    1900 *Congrès International d'Anthropologie et Archéologie*, LIX, p. 427.

Walbank, F. A.
    1957 *Hist. Comm. on Polybuis*, vols. 1 & 2 (Oxford, 1957), revised and reprinted, 1967.

Weingrod, Alex
    1968 "Patrons, Patronage, and Political Parties," *Comparative Studies in Society and History*, vol. 10; p. 1-22.

Weisberg, David B.
    1967 *Guild Structure and Political Allegiance in Early Achaemenid Mesopotamia.* Yale U. Press, New Haven & London.

Wolf, Eric R.
    1966 "Kinship, Friendship and Patron-Client Relations in Complex Societies," in: *Social Anthropology of Complex Socieites*, ed. by Michael Banton.

www.ingramcontent.com/pod-product-compliance
Lightning Source LLC
LaVergne TN
LVHW020323180426
836712LV00011B/137